Jack Nicklaus'
Playing Lessons

Jack Nicklaus' Playing Lessons

By Jack Nicklaus
With Ken Bowden

Illustrated by Jim McQueen

Based on the Golf Digest Playing Lesson Series

Published by Golf Digest/Tennis Inc.,
A New York Times Company
5520 Park Avenue
P.O. Box 0395
Trumbull, Connecticut 06611-0395

Trade book distribution by
Simon and Schuster, A Division
of Simon & Schuster, Inc.
Simon & Schuster Building
Rockefeller Center
1230 Avenue of the Americas
New York, New York 10020

Sixth printing
Third paperback printing
ISBN: 0-914178-60-1 (Paper)
Library of Congress: 80-84953
Printed in the United States
of America

Cover and book design by
Dorothy Geiser
Printing and binding by
Kingsport Press an Arcata Company

Photo Credits
United Press International: page 126 (left)
Courtesy of Jack Nicklaus: 126 (right), 127
    (left), 128 (left), 129
Wide World Photos: 127 (right), 132, 133,
    135, 136, 137, 139, 140, 141, 142, 143
Derek Murray: 130
Toronto Star Syndicate: 131
Frank Gardner: 134
E.D. Lacey: 138

Dedication

To Jack Grout, as fine a friend as a man could have, without whose early guidance and continuing help, none of this would have been possible.

Introduction

I started playing and competing at golf when I was 10. By the time I was 19 I'd had enough success in the amateur game to convince me that I was ready to move up to the pros. In some respects this wasn't just youthful bigheadedness. I could move the ball a healthy distance, and more or less in the desired direction most of the time and there wasn't too much rough in Ohio that I couldn't bulldoze my way out of, and for spells at least I was sheer magic with the putter. Thus, when I turned professional at 21, I had little concern about making a decent living from the game.

It would be fair to say that my awakening was fairly rude.

The first thing I learned out there on the pro tour, where the conditions aren't always quite the same as at Scioto Country Club, was that by play-for-pay standards I couldn't chip worth a darn, nor pitch the ball a whole lot better. Also, my sand play left a lot to be desired whenever the bunkers were powdery, and I couldn't keep the ball low in wind, and I couldn't move it from right to left with any kind of control, and . . . Well, basically what I found out — and quickly — was that if I was ever going to achieve the goals I had in mind, then

I still had a lot of things to learn about hitting a golf ball.

That was lesson one. Lesson two was even sharper.

As an amateur my tournaments usually were fairly widely spaced, leaving plenty of time for work on my game between events. On the pro tour, if you play a full schedule, as I then needed and wanted to do, there is very little time (or energy) left to perform serious surgery on your swing. Essentially, you have to play with whatever you've got that week — have to make the best of your action whether it's healthy or ailing. Also, in amateur golf there were maybe six or eight fellows who could beat me at any given time. On the pro tour there were eighty at least, and more coming along fast all the time. These factors combined caused some very serious reflection about the qualities needed to excel at the game at the major league level.

I had always realized that golf is a two-part game: striking the ball and managing yourself and the course. Like most amateurs, however, I'd worked hardest during my learning years on part one, chiefly because that obviously comes first and is the most fun, but also, I realize in retrospect, because there simply wasn't the intensity of competition or win-to-eat motivation in the amateur game to force a maximum effort on part two.

Probably it was the recognition of my shot-making limitations that brought part two of the game into such sharp focus when I became a pro. Knowing the gaps would take time to fill, I realized that to win in this league with my present weaponry would require a much more thoughtful and strategical approach than I had needed to apply as an amateur. When it paid off fairly quickly I naturally intensified the effort, to the point where it soon became habitual. And for that I am most thankful, because I'm in no doubt today that my record in golf rests much more on part two of the game than on part one.

Now, let's not kid ourselves. Shot-making — ball-striking — comes first and always will. To play strategical and tactical golf you have to be able to hit the ball more or less in a predictable direction a good part of the time. So, if your game is still at the scatter-gun stage, a couple of lessons from a good teacher would probably help you more than this book. Scatter-gunners apart, however, I believe what follows could be of real value to any golfer who is seriously interested in scoring better — and for very little if any extra time on the practice tee. And here's the reason.

As a handicap golfer you are always being told you would score better if you would think more about strategy and less about the swing — to put tactics ahead of technique when actually playing on the course. This is almost certainly true, but as a piece of advice it's pretty useless unless you know or can discover exactly *how* to do that. Unfortunately, as I discovered, no one is born with such knowledge, any more than they are with the feel of a good swing — both have to be learned. And here's the real rub: almost all golf instruction, both direct and written, focuses almost entirely on striking the ball rather than playing the game. In short, golfers suffer from too much information about its physical elements and too little information about the mental qualities necessary to use these to maximum effect.

The recognition of this imbalance some years ago by the editors of *Golf Digest* was what prompted them to ask me to prepare the series of "Playing Lessons" that now form this book. In them I have tried to set down, as simply and specifically as possible, all I have learned in my 30-year love affair with golf about the art and craft of actually *playing* it. Because ball-striking and strategy obviously intertwine, there is a good deal in here about technique, especially as it relates to special shots and recovery play. But the substance of the book is about self-management and course-management, about strategy and tactics — the ultimate keys to scoring at golf.

I hope you enjoy the book, and I hope it helps you to get even more enjoyment and fulfillment from the greatest game of all.

JACK NICKLAUS
January, 1981

Contents

Lifetime Records

Part I
The Inner Game

How to Motivate Yourself to Improve

The two things that motivate me most are closely allied. They are failure and a desire for self-improvement.

By failure, I don't necessarily mean getting beat, although that's often the end result and in itself is a strong motivation to go to work. The kind of failing I'm talking about is failing to measure up to the standards I've set for myself personally. When that happens, I get an irresistible urge—almost a compulsion—to improve. Whatever effort is necessary to prevent another failure, I just *have* to make it. Like now. *Today.*

Frankly, I believe this, more than anything else, is the reason I am where I am today. I'm not an easily satisfied person. Sure I take a lot of satisfaction in what I've achieved. But life doesn't stand still. Every satisfaction wanes after a while, so if you're like me you don't sit around looking backwards. You try to move on, to look for something that gives you another satisfaction and, at the same time, hopefully adds a

I am easily embarrassed by myself. No single emotion is more responsible for whatever I have achieved.

little more to your life.

I've been very satisfied by winning 19 major championships, but I've been satisfied with the *way* I won them only on about half those occasions. A lot of the times I haven't really *won:* what I've *really* done is failed a little less than the other people who had a chance to win. Now, maybe there are people who can get a total kick out of that; who can bury their own fallibility beneath a pure glow of winning. I'd have to believe that a lot of the really talented one-time winners in the history of sports maybe had something of that in them.

Not me. Strange as it may seem, I sometimes go through a sort of psychic downer after a big win. Once all the razzmatazz and euphoria have worn off, my mind gets back to all the mistakes I made that might have caused me *not* to win. And that's a goad. That motivates me.

I said in my book *Golf My Way* that I know I shall never play perfect golf. But that knowledge does not stop me from *trying* to play perfectly. There never has been a round—much less a tournament—that has absolutely, totally, 100 percent satisfied *me* personally. And *that* motivates me.

I'm not trying to mechanize my game, to turn myself into some kind of automaton. No golfer can help making mistakes—lots of them. That's the nature of the game—and part of its challenge and charm, too. What I'm talking about is not attaining true perfection, which is unrealistic, but simply continuing to improve, which is extremely realizable. In short, my goal is to achieve more often what I know mentally I can do physically.

At my point in golf, the problem is not automating a swing or a set of playing techniques. For better or worse my full swing was "grooved"—as far as anybody's swing can be grooved—when I was 13. And, on anything short of a full swing, you don't "groove" technique: what you do is develop a whole range of special techniques based on a few fundamental principles. So far as pure technique goes, my problem is primarily to keep what I have at the highest possible peak. You don't do that by learning a new set of tricks. You do it by continual adjustment within the framework of what experience has taught you are the proper fundamentals.

So here's my problem—and my strongest motivation. During more than 20 years of tournament golf I have at one point or another succeeded in playing just about every shot that is actually playable. Sometimes I've had a comparatively high degree of success, as with long irons. Sometimes I've had what I believe to be a poor ratio of success, as with chipping and, at one time, sand play. But *I have played all the shots successfully,* whether it be once or 10,000 times.

Now, obviously I know that I will never *always* play them all successfully—we've been into that. But what I do want to do—what deeply motivates me—is to *continually improve my rate of success at them.* To put it another way, I want to constantly minimize my rate of failure at playing shots that my intellect tells me and my experience proves to me I can physically play near-perfectly.

Motivationally, this urge for self-improvement has very little to do with winning, and nothing at all to do with making money or other materialistic factors. I've always believed that *performance* takes care of those things.

Anytime there's a cooling off in this impulse to improve, one emotion above all others will get a good blaze going again. It's embarrassment. I am extremely easily embarrassed by myself. No single emotion is more responsible for whatever I've achieved.

Probably my most traumatic experience—and I've had a lot of them—came on the 16th hole at Medinah in the U.S. Open one year. Standing on the tee, I had an excellent chance of winning the championship, which I wanted as much as I've ever wanted anything, not only for its own sake but because it also would have been the second leg of the Grand Slam. Oddly enough, I love the hole—I think it's probably the best hole at Medinah.

The ideal tee shot for me on this 452-yard par-4 is a fade down the left side, cutting the ball back to the center or right center of the fairway to set up the easiest approach angle. That's the shot I planned. I've hit it perfectly a million times. It's my bread-and-butter shot; the "shape" I've been driving with more than 90 percent of the time over 20 years of tournament golf. This time I pull-hooked the ball dead

There's an awful lot more to learning to hit good golf shots than belting out a few million balls.

left, deep into the trees.

I knew immediately where it was going ,and I knew that, with the swing pattern I had going, I should have tried a knock-down, controlled drive. That purely mental error had a strong motivating effect on me afterwards, because never before had I been so embarrassed on a golf course as I was on that hole and the remaining two holes. When I got off the 18th green I decided right then that I was never going to embarrass myself that badly again.

We needn't get into what this reaction produced in terms of mental and physical effort, but I can say that, even though I've never been busier in my life with non-golf work and worries, the rest of that season didn't turn out too shabbily.

OK. My chief motivations are dislike of failure, an urge for constant self-improvement and a hatred of embarrassing myself. How can a handicap golfer relate to these things?

Well, let's start with a truism that is critical to all of these motivations—and, indeed, to this entire series of lessons. No matter how motivated you already are as a golfer, or want to become, it isn't going to move you one step forward if you can't hit a golf ball half-way decently. Neither are all the other big words, like dedication and determination and confidence and concentration and commitment and so on.

Even though by nature you may have all these in spades, the only way you can capitalize on them in golf is through the shots you hit. If you can't hit the shots, you're a dead duck in terms of applying your temperamental attributes to the game.

The answer, obviously, is to become a better shot-maker. And how do you do that? Obviously, through practice. But there's really an awful lot more to learning to hit good golf shots than belting out a few million balls.

The first thing you need is a crystal clear under-standing of what you are fundamentally trying to achieve when you swing a golf club. Very few club golfers have this. One reason may be that, until recent times, comparatively few teachers have conveyed the cause-and-effect, ballistic and geometrical factors of the club's impact on the ball.

Perhaps a more likely reason is that most golfers can't be bothered with these seemingly boring "theoretical" basics, any more than they can with the grip and set-up fundamentals that are responsible for close to 90 percent of good golf technique. Either way, the result is that most golfers are like a guy driving a car who doesn't know where he's going or what he wants to do when he gets there. They spend all their time on the mechanics of motion without knowing the *objectives* of moving.

Find a good teaching professional, have him explain these cause-and-effect principles, and study them until they are mentally ingrained to the point where they automatically become the objective of every swing you make. If you cannot find such a teacher, then find a book or magazine that will give you this information. Even that's a heck of a lot better than continuing to call yourself a golfer without really knowing what you have to do at impact to become one.

Another thought I'd like to put in your head about shotmaking concerns consistency. The reason you don't play as well as the tour pros isn't that you can't ever hit a good shot. Everybody who breaks 90 *some-times* hits shots as good as me or any other pro, even though maybe only once in a great while. Obviously, these super shots aren't your problem— but neither, in one sense, are your absolutely diabolical shots. *Your problem, at your level of golf, is the enormous gap between your best shots and your worst shots.* If you could close that gap even a little bit, your golf *scores* would improve out of all recognition.

And that brings us back to my primary motivational factor. In order not to embarrass myself, I seek constant self-improvement. I do so basically by trying to narrow the gap between my best shots and my worst shots. In my case, the gap may not be that wide, but the principle is the same. I do it not by looking for a new "secret," or trying to swing like Ben Hogan, but by studying and work on what I already possess, or am certain I can develop. In short, I stay within my own capabilities.

You may not win the Grand Slam by doing the same, or even your club championship. But if you made the same sort of effort, I *know* you'd become a better golfer. All it takes to make the effort is motivation. ∎

Inner Game 2:

How to Get Yourself Mentally Ready to Play

I guess I'm lucky in that I don't need to become some sort of recluse to play my best golf. I don't need to go away and hide from the world. I'm simply not made that way. I certainly couldn't function like, say, Muhammad Ali, who seems to become more invincible the closer commotion gets to pandemonium. But neither could I function like, say, Ben Hogan, who seemed to need almost total isolation to play his best. What I need most in preparing mentally for any tournament is simply my own kind of normality.

In recent years whenever I've slumped, a lot of people who don't know me very well—including some writers—have put it down to overexertion in other areas—such as business, or course design, or building a golf club and running a golf tournament. Well, the answer to that is that I've probably never had a better golfing year than 1975, which happened to be the busiest year of my life in terms of business, course design, building Muirfield Village Golf Club and organizing the Memorial Tournament there.

I sometimes get criticism from people who do know me well that other aspects of my life are so debilitating that they detract from golf. Generally they are talking about the amount of extra traveling I do to be at home as much as possible, and the amount of time and energy I spend doing things with the kids, and the effort I make to play and watch other sports—in short, to live as full a family life as possible. Here again, I don't think I'd have been any more successful at golf if I'd adopted a different life style.

I think there are basically three reasons why this

The most important thing for me in preparing for major tournaments is basic peace of mind.

busy and varied life style works for me.

The first is that I am temperamentally unsuited to a one-track life. Golf is my love and my career, but it never has been and never could be *everything*. As a result, I have always tried a lot of other things, and as time has passed I have been fortunate enough to find that the four main activities that have evolved each fulfills a basic need.

First, of course, there is my family, which fulfills my strongest emotional needs. Next, there is golf course design, which supplies an outlet for creativity. Then there is business, which poses intellectual and competitive challenges totally different from those of golf. Finally, there are other sports, which provide both physical exercise and mental relaxation.

All these things in sum provide one further ingredient, which is absolutely essential to my mental attitude as a golfer. That fifth ingredient is the stimulus—really, the constant freshening—of my desire to play tournament golf. In other words, after an intensive effort in any or all of these other areas, I am always eager to get back to actually playing golf—just like the weekend golfer who can't wait to get to the course on Saturday morning after a week of living his "other" lives.

Without these alternatives, I believe I would very quickly become stale with golf; would lack the mental freshness that is so essential to competitive drive. And I also believe—although it's none of my business how other people live their lives—that a lot of tour golfers might play better if they could approach the game a little more this way.

The second reason why this varied life style seems to work in my case is that I am, by nature, a pretty organized person. I like and seek order and system, and as life has become busier I've become better at self-organization. Without that personality trait I probably couldn't cope, but with it I have been able to handle in any given day what might create instant nervous collapse in another type of personality. And I also happen to believe that my organized nature is a great asset on the golf course itself.

An ability to identify and be decisive about priorities is the third reason why there hasn't been a need to make golf the be-all and end-all of life. For example, there are times when, even with plenty of energy and organization, the whole scene begins to get out of hand —as after that awful 82 I had in the final round of the Crosby in 1976. Luckily, when that happens I have so far had the inner strength to quickly do whatever I believe is necessary to right the situation. After the Crosby and the Hope that year, the necessary thing to do was to cut right back on everything except golf. That's exactly what I did, and the result was a victory in the Tournament Players Championship.

That then is my overall mental approach to golf. What about more specific mental preparation for tournaments, rounds and shots?

The most important thing to me in preparing for major tournaments—say the U.S. and British Opens— is basic peace of mind. By this I don't mean the elimination of *all* concerns and worries, because anyone with any intelligence realizes early in life that that is simply not possible. What I mean is having done all that I'm capable of to solve any really major problems that may be facing me or those close to me.

As an example of a problem that would affect me mentally going into a big tournament, take the new irons I began using one year after nine years without a change. These clubs grew out of a longtime determination that whatever went on the market with my name on it would eventually be exactly what I had designed and actually played.

At first, even after two years of development and even though they were excellent clubs, these irons were not *exactly* right for me when I started playing them at the beginning of the year. This meant in my mind that they could not therefore be exactly right for everyone else.

The result was that they *had* to be made right, as I saw rightness, not only for me to play with, and not only for the company to be able to market them honestly as Nicklaus clubs, but for the sake of everyone else who decided to buy them because of that name and imprint.

Now, the clubs may still not be right for everyone who does buy them, because it's impossible to design one club for all golfers, but that isn't the point. The point is that I had to feel that everything that possibly could be done had been done to make them as right as they could be by my standards and experience. So I gave a great deal of effort to achieving that goal between the Crosby and the Masters. In the final analysis, of course, it wasn't only for the reasons I've outlined. If I hadn't resolved the problem, I would have gone to Augusta with the handicap of a nagging mental worry.

Examples of what I mean by emotional peace of mind are less easy to find, but perhaps the best one concerns my family. We've made it a rule ever since schooling prevented our children from always traveling with us on tour that I am never away from home for more than two weeks at a time. So far I have never broken it, and to start doing so now would definitely upset me—and, I think, the entire family.

In terms of specifics, rather than overall mood, my mental preparation for an important tournament hasn't changed much since becoming a professional. I spend a lot of time thinking about the golf course that we shall be playing, going over it mentally hole by hole and shot by shot, and recalling past experiences there, until I have a clear picture of the ideal way to tackle it.

The two or three days I almost always spend playing the course the week before the tournament are used to confirm or correct these judgments, and to work on my game. Being 100 percent prepared in

I never hit a shot, even in practice, without having a very sharp, in-focus picture of it in my head.

these areas is critical to my peace of mind. Beyond these factors, all I basically seek in the way of mental preparation is normality, which is achieved simply by living my usual life style.

So much for pre-tournament preparation. What about pre-round preparation?

Once again, there's nothing dramatic to report— no "secrets." At tournaments I try to adopt the same life style we follow at home, which is one reason we almost always rent a house for the major championships. I don't go into a shell or anything like that. As a family, we eat the same, sleep the same, talk the same, play the same, goof around and laugh the same as we do at home. Relatives and friends come around, and we go around to see them. There are certain little rituals we follow—superstitions I guess you'd call them —like Barbara taking her special omelette pan everywhere. But basically we are just ourselves.

External distractions seem to get minimized simply because the people around me are more thoughtful at big events, but no special barricades are erected. I may think more about golf, but we don't talk about it any more than we normally do—which is very little. I don't think I get any more short-tempered or withdrawn or moody than I normally am—although Barbara would have to speak about that.

In short, we all simply go on behaving as we normally do. Maybe one reason for this is that as much as I and those around me want me to win, we know it isn't going to be the end of the world if I don't.

In terms of mental preparation at the course itself, once again my basically organized temperament has been a big help all through my career. So has the ability to quickly switch concentration from one subject to another and lock totally on whatever presently demands maximum attention.

On the way to the course with Barbara we might talk about family matters, or what we're going to have for dinner, or where she's going shopping before or after the round. If I'm driving out with associates, we'll generally either just kid around or get deep into some business situation or problem. We've made a lot of decisions on the way to tournaments.

I guess I'm able to switch on and off like this because, once I arrive at the course and step out of the car, I know exactly what I am going to do and am able at that moment to lock totally into it mentally. From that moment on, the priority is playing golf. For the next five or six hours there is a routine to be followed that has proved effective over a period of more than 20 years, and with which I am mentally familiar and comfortable.

Generally at a major tournament I will have practiced after the previous day's round, working on what I learned about my swing or putting action during actual play. This is the most valuable practice I ever do, because it is so intensely related to what occurred during the heat of competition.

Once I've broken down the muscular adhesions with some easy exercises and a few short shots, I will go back to what I was working on the previous evening. Hopefully how the ball behaves will reinforce what I had then determined both mentally and physically about my game. If so, confident that I have solved a basic problem or established a basically sound pattern (if only temporarily, golf being what it is!), I will move on to play the variety of shots that I believe will be needed on the course that day. Here the objective is not simply to build confidence by performing the shots physically, but to mentally re-identify, rehearse and re-absorb the patterns and feels that make them happen.

Once on the golf course, my overall frame of mind depends a lot on what I have learned from the practice session. If I'm comfortable with the shotmaking factors, then I can concentrate exclusively on the strategical factors presented by each hole and shot. This is when I feel the most confident, and it is also when golf is the greatest fun, because then one can attempt to play the ideal shot in every situation. In golf there *is* an ideal shot in every situation, and I can almost always identify it. What I get absolutely no fun from is knowing the ideal shot but not being able to attempt it because of some problem in my swing. The fact that I have so often attempted to play such a shot when realistically I should not have done so has cost me a great many tournaments.

Irrespective of how I am swinging or stroking, my mental preparation for each individual shot is very specific and highly "programmed." We described this process fully in the book *Golf My Way,* and I don't think I could do it better in different words. Here's what we said:

"I never hit a shot, even in practice, without having a very sharp, in-focus picture of it in my head. It's like a color movie. First I *see* the ball where I want it to finish, nice and white and sitting up high on the bright green grass. Then the scene quickly changes and I *see* the ball going there: its path, trajectory and shape, even its behavior on landing. Then there's a sort of fadeout, and the next scene shows me making the kind of swing that will turn the previous image into reality. Only at the end of this short, private, Hollywood spectacular do I select a club and step up to the ball.

"It may be that handicap golfers also 'go to the movies' like this before most of their shots, but somehow I doubt it. Frequently those I play with in pro-ams seem to have the club at the ball and their feet planted before they start *seeing* pictures in their mind's eye. Maybe even then they see only pictures of the swing, rather than what it's supposed to achieve. If that's true in your case, then I believe a few moments of movie-making might work some small miracles in your game. Just make sure your movies show a perfect shot. We don't want any horror films of shots flying into sand or water or out-of-bounds." ■

J. McQueen

Inner Game 3:

What You Can Learn from the Mental Errors of the Pros

The No. 1 mental fault on the tour—and one I'm frequently guilty of—is the same as the No. 1 fault in club golf: trying to play beyond one's capabilities.

A classic example in my own case occurred one year at the Crosby. After two months of playing hardly any golf, I scored very well the first two rounds. Somewhere around the middle of the third round, it began to come home to me that I wasn't really mentally or physically ready to win a tournament. Although I led at the end of 54 holes, I'd begun to realize on the back nine of the third round that my game wasn't physically sharp enough to play some of the shots that my mind suggested. I got away with it on the front nine in the final round, but on the back, under the pressure, I let myself fall into the trap of trying to do things that I simply wasn't in shape to do: attempting shots out of my imagination that I hadn't practiced for a couple of months, instead of playing the less-than-ideal shots I knew I could play.

This happens all the time on the tour, just as it does among weekend golfers, and particularly among the younger and less experienced players. You'll often see one of these fellows get himself into a position to win after two or three rounds, then play badly. He doesn't

A lot of times you don't actually win so much as all the other guys lose.

play badly because he's a poor golfer—he had to be a good player to get himself into contention. The reason he plays badly is that he doesn't yet have the experience to think and act totally objectively under pressure, with the result that he tries to do more with the shots than he's actually capable of doing. And this becomes a vicious circle, because, when you start to make mistakes, very often—even with great experience —you begin to place even heavier demands on your game to try to hit shots that will make up for those mistakes.

Lack of patience
Another mental failing on tour—and even worse in club golf—is closely related to what we've just been talking about, and that is lack of patience. It may have become a cliche, but it is absolutely true that you cannot *force* a good golf score, and especially not a *winning* golf score. The best you can do in golf is to identify the most effective shot you believe you can play in any given situation (which, by the way, is an art form in itself), and then make your very best try to execute it. Some of those shots will come off, and some of them won't, and you need a great deal of patience to understand and accept that fact. If you don't—if you lack patience—then you're on the way to desperation, or at least overaggression, and that's never won any tournaments that I've been a part of.

Being overaggressive
Overaggressiveness is another common fault on tour, and I think it's sometimes born of a lack of understanding among the younger or less thoughtful players that you need more than a good golf swing to win tournaments—you also need *experience.* Often a fellow comes out and he's been a hotshot amateur or college player, and he's got such confidence and wants to win so badly that all he can think of is "Attack!" But the tour is, first of all, a different league, and, second, it's a game in which a lot of times you don't actually win so much as all the other guys lose.

You have to be able to recognize when 71 is a heck of a fine score, and when 68 isn't all that much of a score. You have to be able to read conditions and interpret a scoreboard. In short, you have to know when to be aggressive and when not to be aggressive. Even Arnold Palmer at his boldest played within these parameters—in fact, Arnie has admitted it was one of the toughest lessons he had to learn.

Failure to "manage" the course
Along the same lines—and again it's basically a matter of learning by experience—you have to know how to *play* a golf course: "manage" it is probably as good a word as any. An awful lot of golfers out on tour have never really learned how to do that. The simplest examples of the kind of thing I'm talking about are knowing when—and why—to hit, say, a 3-iron off a

tee instead of a driver, or a particular type of approach shot in relation to the severity of a hazard, or a certain type of shot from a particular kind of sand. All the very best players are expert in such matters, whereas I sometimes have the feeling with less successful players that, because they are professionals, they're somehow embarrassed to hit less than a driver on a par-4 hole or shoot other than at the stick on a dangerous pin position.

Practicing without a specific purpose
Another common mental mistake on tour—and yet again it's mirrored by the handicap golfer—is what you might call the ball-beating syndrome. There's little doubt that, at the formative stage of one's game as a youngster, it's almost impossible to hit too many golf balls. But once a golfer has developed a basically sound game overall, real progress depends much more on the *quality* rather than the quantity of practice. In other words, hitting balls can only produce improvement when you practice something *very specific,* which obviously means that you have to have mentally determined what you are going to practice, and why you are going to practice it, before you start hitting.

That's why I always achieve my most productive practice after an actual round. Then the mistakes are fresh in my mind, and I can go to the practice tee and work specifically on those mistakes. Often I carry this even to the point of writing both the fault and the correction down on paper for future reference, and at worst I'll tell my caddie, Angelo, "Tomorrow before I start practicing, remind me about my head," or my grip, or hips, or whatever it is I've been working on.

Very frequently on tour you'll see the less experienced players giving each other lessons, and it always concerns me to see how quickly some of them will accept advice from others. Certainly such advice is offered in a spirit of friendship or from genuine interest in another's problems, but it always has to be treated very circumspectly, simply because what works for one golfer doesn't work for all others.

Along the same lines, I think most of the greatest golfers down the years have recognized that it's impossible to forever "groove" a particular pattern of play, either by ball-beating or any other means. Given a basically effective swing, what they've done is continually work on a variety of specific modifications to temporarily achieve a particular desired result, while accepting mentally that the result always will be temporary—that slight modifications always will be necessary. Then, once a particular result is achieved on the practice tee, this realism frees them from the sort of mental compulsion to go on hitting balls that can arise from the belief that if you hit enough you'll turn into some sort of machine.

Playing too much and growing stale
Another mistake on tour—and probably one the

I'm a firm believer in the theory that people do their best at things they enjoy.

average golfer would like to have the time to make—is playing too much golf, both competitively and during what is supposed to be free time. Every tour golfer has an obligation to the sponsors to play in a reasonable number of tournaments, but in the final analysis the first obligation has to be to oneself, if only because overextension invariably reduces performance, which isn't in anyone's best interests.

There never has been a golfer who can play at his or her peak all the time, which means that to have peaks you must accept valleys. I think much of my success stems from the fact that I not only accept valleys, but actually make them for myself by regularly forgetting golf and working or playing at a variety of totally different things. But the valleys aren't wasted in a golfing sense, because I use them to build myself up and prepare mentally for the next peak. In short, I point myself to peak at certain times—to meet clearly defined goals—and use the rest of the time as recuperative and build-up periods.

One reason a lot of tour players can't make themselves do this is that they are scared they'll lose their games if they lay off golf for any length of time. I think this reasoning is fallacious. A long-honed talent doesn't go away when it is rested—in fact, very often it reconstitutes itself. Certainly there'll be a need for some fine tuning when the game is resumed, but a layoff usually stimulates one to work hard at this, and in a very fresh and positive frame of mind.

Thinking about the money instead of the shot

Obviously, it's easier for me financially to take this approach than it is for some players, but it's the pattern I followed long before I could rest easy about money. And the same is true about what seems to me another common mental mistake on tour: thinking about golf in terms of money rather than first and foremost as a game.

Perhaps because I was lucky enough to play a lot as an amateur, golf has always been essentially a game to me, even though I've earned my living at it for 15 or so years. The result has been that I've always been able to totally enjoy golf for its own sake—and I'm a firm believer in the theory that people only do their best at things they truly enjoy.

By having fun playing golf, I was—and still am—inspired to do my best at it, and by giving of my best I was fortunate enough to make a good living. Had I taken a different approach—the how-much-per-shot approach you sometimes see on tour—I'm sure I'd have been a lot less successful. And the reason is very simple: if you are thinking "This could be worth $20,000" as you're standing over a winning putt on the 72nd hole, first you're adding enormously to the already powerful pressure on your nervous system, and secondly there is no way your mind can focus as totally and clearly on *how* you're going to sink that putt as it must to enable you to do so. In short, what

I'm saying is that thinking about playing and competing is what makes money—or wins trophies—in golf, not thinking about the *results* of winning.

Accepting too many social invitations

Another problem that the best players are always on guard against—and it's one of the most difficult to avoid—is getting so caught up in the tour as a way of life that it actually drags you down as a person and as an athlete. What I'm really talking about here are the social pressures of tournament golf, which can be very diverting and debilitating. If the tour is totally your life—as it is for many players—then it's only human to want some part of it to be whoopee-type fun, especially as almost everyone else but the players seem to have all the whoopee-type fun they can handle. What a lot of these friendly and enthusiastic people around golf tournaments sometimes lose sight of is that golf is no different from any other sport in that the performer has to train for it physically and mentally. And what some of the golfers they are so eager to entertain fail to recognize is that the week of a tournament is the willing host's big event of the year, whereas for the player it happens 20 or 30 or even 40 times a year. Every athlete has to let loose once in a while, because it would be a dull and dreary existence without an occasional party. Where the danger lies is in getting into the habit of accepting *every* drink that is offered, and *every* dinner date, and *every* trip to someone's favorite nightspot.

This sort of thing is particularly a danger with guys who deep down aren't happy with the kind of life forced on them by the tour—and there are a lot of guys like that. They may be unhappy with some element of their family life, bored and restless in the long hours between playing, tired from too much golf, vaguely or consciously aware that they're missing something in life by dedicating themselves so much to golf. In other words, they're less than content with themselves, unable to "find" themselves other than when they're actually on the golf course—and sometimes not even then.

If a psychiatrist were to analyze most of the fellows on the tour, I think he'd find that the guys who are not like this are the ones who've established other values and other lives beyond golf. I think one thing all of them have in common is the ability to put first things first, which leads to the recognition that golf—or any single activity—can never give a normal human being total satisfaction, no matter how good he may be at it or how strong his ambition to be good at it. Most of the successful and contented guys on tour have sound marriages, and nice families, and a few real friends rather than a thousand acquaintances, and some deep interests in things totally removed from golf, like Arnold and his flying and Gary Player and his quarter horses and Gene Littler and his antique cars.

In short, they have things in perspective. ∎

What You Can Learn from the Mental Errors of Amateurs

Not being a teacher, and having a different set of golfing problems than most handicap players, it's not easy for me to advise you about specific mental approaches to the game. That's why, in most of this series, I've basically discussed my own mental approach, leaving the reader to select whatever he or she thinks might be useful.

However, I do play with golfers of all levels in pro-ams, and I see more and more amateur competition gallerying my older boys. So here are a few thoughts on some specific mental factors that relate to most handicap golfers.

Unless you play golf purely for exercise, don't ever practice without first working out mentally exactly *why* you are practicing. If you aren't clear about that, don't go out and beat 800 balls a day in the hope that a miracle will occur, because, even if you do stumble across "a way," it won't last more than a matter of hours if you don't understand the *reason* it works. Instead, go and get some professional help, and keep

Don't try to build a new golf swing, or remake your old one, during pre-round practice.

getting it until you fully grasp the *reasons* for holding and swinging a golf club in a particular way.

Don't try to build a new golf swing, or remake your old one, during pre-round practice. The time to make radical swing changes is during extended practice sessions that will not be followed immediately by serious play on the course. Any major change not fully assimilated in practice will almost certainly break down under the pressure of trying to score well. The result usually is even more confusion and frustration than you suffer trying to make an imperfect but familiar swing work. The object of pre-round practice is simply to loosen up the muscles, develop tempo and find the best swing feel and/or mental swing image for that day's play.

Build a storehouse of key swing thoughts

Every tour player has a stock of key swing thoughts that he'll draw on as necessary to keep his game in synch. Generally one will emerge from his mental storehouse during pre-round practice, and he'll stick with it at least for that particular day. Try to build up your own stock of key thoughts and feels, drawing them from your best shot-making periods. Write them down if that's the only way you can remember them. But be disciplined about how many of them you use on the course. Most people can only concentrate well on one thought at a time.

Under pressure, play your proven shot

Irrespective of your level of shotmaking ability, you definitely will give yourself the best chance under pressure by sticking with the kind of swing and shots' that you have played predominantly in the past. When the squeeze is on, don't suddenly try to play way above your usual standards by inventing a whole new method. Whatever your "A-to-B" shot may be, go with it when the chips are down. If it's a slice, and you think you can get the ball more or less into the proper position with it, go ahead and play a slice, instead of suddenly trying to invent a nice little draw. Stay with whatever you know from past experience you have the best chance of executing by instinct and reflex.

Think more about tactics than swing

The less you can think about how you are going to swing the club until you're actually called upon to do so, the more mental energy you will have available for managing your play and the better you'll score. Management in golf consists simply of observing the topographical and climatic characteristics of a hole, analyzing the best way to play it in relation to those characteristics and your own capabilities, and then mentally reviewing how you'll execute the appropriate shot before you do. Constantly thinking about the third of these factors decreases your ability to think about the first two, which are the *absolute keys* to scoring well. In other words, you're going about golf backwards. A glaring example of this approach is the guy who makes a perfect swing and a great hit, but with the wrong club and faulty alignment, and then wonders why the ball finishes in the woods short and wide of the green. He's so bound up in his swing he has no mental resources left to assess what he's trying to make his swing do.

Let your mind rest between shots

Understand that concentration isn't an all-out effort all the time, but simply an intense mental bearing down on the playing and planning of each shot as it arises. That's why, cliché or not, it's true that you can only play golf "one shot at a time." I certainly don't "think golf" all the time. I let my mind rest between shots by allowing it to focus lightly on whatever non-golfing subjects it chooses, and I think you'll play better if you do the same.

Don't try shots beyond your capability

Be realistic. There are shots you probably can play, there are shots you might occasionally be able to play, and there are shots you definitely *cannot* play. I don't think I can recall a pro-am in which at least one amateur did not try to play at least one shot that was absolutely beyond his capabilities. And I can recall a lot of amateur partners who tried repeatedly to play shots beyond *anyone's* capabilities. That's dumb, not only in terms of the immediate affect on your score, but also in terms of your confidence.

What is realistic? If you have a 14 handicap, then on a par-72 course a score somewhere between 82 and 90 is realistic. Trying to play as though you are a 76 shooter not only is unrealistic, but generally will result in a score closer to 96. The key to playing realistically is not so much playing conservatively when in trouble, as avoiding trouble in the first place by accepting what the scoreboard tells you before you tee off. Any time the stroke rating of a hole is lower than your handicap, *your* par in fact is a bogey. That doesn't mean you shouldn't try for a par, but it does mean that you shouldn't *expect* to par that hole

Improving at the game lies in narrowing the margin between your best and your worst shots.

consistently until you've done the homework that will make you a better shotmaker and a lower handicapper.

Here's another way to play golf realistically. You'll grant that every shot in golf possesses a certain risk factor. Obviously, the degree of risk depends on each person's shotmaking ability, but from experience everyone can roughly grade his own risk factors. Let's designate "A" for high risk, "B" for medium, and "C" for low risk. Applying these gradings, a realistic golfer would attempt an "A" shot only when he was playing particularly well, he would go for the "B" shot most of the time, and he would always opt for the "C" shot when playing poorly. If your biggest golfing problem is two or three disasters a round, give this approach a try.

Aim to peak your game for your big tournaments
Another form of realism is accepting the fact that your game is always going to go through peaks and valleys —absolute consistency of performance is impossible. This is a particularly tough thing for some of the good young tour players to accept. After a hot run some of them get down on themselves too much when they cool off, and I suspect a lot of handicap golfers are the same way. The answer is to try to control your performance cycles rather than fight them. Aim to peak at certain times for certain events and accept the fact you're not at your best at other times. In my case the effort generally has been to peak for the major championships and maybe a couple more tournaments each year. In yours, it might be the member-guest and the club championship. You might not win, of course, as I have failed to win more often than not, but you stand a far better chance that way than trying to reach a peak in the spring and hold it for the rest of the year.

Don't let opponents' shots affect you
You probably have noticed that tour players rarely react much to either the good or the bad shots of their playing partners, even when each man in a group is coming to the wire with a winning chance. The reason is that tournament golfers almost always play the course and almost never play the man. This is the best way to approach stroke play, but it's also the soundest strategy in match play most of the time.

Short of deliberate gamesmanship, the only way you can affect an opponent is by the number of shots you hit per hole, and it is the course—not your opponent —that determines how many shots you hit. The more you allow yourself to react emotionally to what someone else is doing, the less cool-headed you'll be in concentrating on what *you* are trying to do. And if there's one mental quality above all others that wins golf tournaments—at stroke or match play—it's cool-headedness when the squeeze is on.

Narrow margin between best and worst shots
It's impossible in golf not to get elated by your own good shots and discouraged by bad ones, but the more of a balance you can maintain between the two emotions, the better you'll score—especially in stroke play. Achieving such a balance requires acceptance of two hard facts about golf. First, golf is not and never will be an entirely "fair" game; there always will be an element of luck beyond your control. Second, being human and therefore fallible, you always are going to hit a percentage of bad shots along with the good shots.

Understand that improving at the game—and winning at it—lies in narrowing the margin between your best and your worst shots. At the club level this is really the only difference between the game of, say, a 4-handicapper and an 8-handicapper, and on the tour it's the only difference between the consistent high finisher and the streaky player.

How to cope with bad breaks
Golf is probably the easiest game in the world to quit at, but it's also the greatest game not to quit at. The most common form of quitting I see, both in tour players and my pro-am partners, is letting adversity —especially bad luck—create mental carelessness. Such a fellow may still try with his swing when he's over the ball, but he's so angry or depressed about whatever mistake he just made or injustice he thinks he suffered that he doesn't try with his head beforehand. The result is even more time in the boondocks, causing more depression and anger, which leads to more time in the tall stuff, until finally the guy gives up altogether and begins to "play hockey."

One thing that has helped me avoid that kind of self-destruction is acceptance of the fact that the good and bad breaks ultimately even out. Another helpful factor has been pride. After having embarrassed myself by messing up a shot or a hole, sheer pride generally makes me try even harder next time simply to prevent embarrassing myself any more. It's an emotion that has caused me not only to hang in hard enough to win a few times when the chance seemed gone, but that also has done a lot to bring me out of some severe shotmaking slumps. ∎

J. McQueen

Inner Game 5:

How to Break the Scoring Barrier of 90 – Repeatedly

Golf calls for two interrelated but distinct skills. One is the ability to strike the ball, to physically play the shots. The other is the ability to observe, evaluate, plan and think your way around the golf course, to play strategically and tactically—in short, to score.

No matter how good you become at the first, you'll never be a successful golfer if you are not equally good at the second. You can, however, become a considerably better player if you can make yourself into a first-rate self-manager and course-manager. I think my own career proves this. Day in, day out, I'm a better strategist and tactician than I am a shotmaker. As a result it's often been said that I have had the ability to win when playing poorly. That actually is not quite the truth. The truth is that I have won many times when I have been *striking* the ball comparatively poorly, but I have never won—not even when striking at my best—when I have been *managing* myself or my game poorly.

It's these mental factors, I believe, that finally determine a person's level of success at golf, whether you measure it by winning major championships or breaking 90. Virtually all of the top forty or fifty players on the pro tour possess comparable shot-making skills, yet only a handful consistently win or finish high. Very

Relate how you are playing to the difficulty factor combined with the potential penalty factor.

simply, they are the best self-managers and course-managers. The same is true of country club golf. In any group with roughly the same shot-making ability, one or two will generally score lower than the others, because they are better mental commanders of themselves and the game.

Don't let me build up your hopes falsely. Breaking 90 takes a certain amount of shot-making skill—the ability to propel the ball in a predominantly forward rather than a sideways direction. If you don't have that ability now, then the only way you're going to get it is by improving your swing technique, which requires knowledge, practice and perhaps instruction from a skilled teacher. However, if you already hit the ball well enough to occasionally break 100, there's a very good chance that you could break 90 without hitting it any better. Let me see if I can show you how.

Everybody gets a kick out of hitting the ball a long way, but a lot of golfers at every level of the game let the desire for that kick destroy their scores. They've never learned—or have ever been able to mentally accept—the fact that golf is a thousand times more a game of precision than of power.

Let me use myself as an example. Swinging at my best, I can drive the ball more or less straight about 260 yards. I am actually physically capable of driving it a good 20 yards farther, but the more I try to do so the greater the chance that I will hit it crooked. Thus I only go for what I would call "unnatural" distance when the potential gain outweighs the risk, as, for example, on a wide open, trouble-free par five. The rest of the time I put precision way ahead of power by playing well within my natural distance capabilities, both from the tees and into the greens.

The probability is that you, if 90 is still your golfing goal, go for "unnatural" distance almost all the time. Whether for reasons of vanity or blind hope, you almost certainly try to hit the ball too hard too often, especially off the tee, with the result that you are very frequently staring at disaster even before you've properly begun the hole.

From my experience in pro-ams, I'd say this was the single biggest score-wrecker among amateurs, the high handicappers. I'd also say that the cure must start with the hardest of all things to achieve on a golf course, which is acceptance of reality—acceptance of your own limitations. You simply may not have the technique to hit the ball as far as you'd like to and still keep it on the golf course. Unpalatable as that fact may be, the sooner you accept it the faster your scores will improve.

Here's a way to convince yourself to do so. Take every club out of the bag until you get to the club with which you feel confident you can generally hit the fairway. Go out and play a couple of rounds alone using this club for tee shots, instead of the driver. If it's a five wood or a four iron, swing it as you would normally try to swing a five wood or a four iron, rather

than whaling away with it as you would with the driver. Then on all approach shots, take *one more* stronger club than you first thought of; that is a six iron instead of a seven—or a five instead of a six. Again: *do not* whale away at the ball.

Having started to play realistically in terms of your distance capability, extend this mental approach to your overall immediate golfing goal.

Accept the fact that if you are now a 100-shooter, you aren't suddenly going to become a 70s-shooter overnight. You may get to that level some day, but your immediate goal must be a realistically reachable one—89 or a couple better. The priority, in going from the low hundreds or high nineties to that level, is not making more birdies and pars, which isn't realistic, but simply reducing the number of flat-out disasters—triple and quadruple bogies—you incur per round. This *is* realistic.

Your mental attitude regarding par will have a high bearing on how successful you are. If your average score is now 100, par for *you* on a hole that's say, 467 yards long, with an out-of-bounds and five bunkers and two water hazards, isn't the four that's marked on the card. It's five—or maybe even six.

Try to play such a hole for a four, and the self-imposed mental pressure, not to mention the physical forcing of shots, is bound to make you highly disaster-prone. Plan and play it for a five or six, and you give yourself an excellent chance of achieving what in effect is your own true par (or better with a good putt), simply by attempting what you are confident is within your capabilities.

The example I've used of a tough par four is applicable on every hole you encounter. Set your own realistic personal par hole-by-hole and you'll be surprised how much your scores improve without any improvement in your overall striking ability.

If too many disasters still keep you on the wrong side of 90, then try this. Give every shot that confronts you, whether from short grass or trouble, a personal difficulty rating of either A, B or C. For example, if you're in rough with a water hazard between you and the green, a three-wood "go-for-it" attempt would be an A shot, a five iron lay-up short of the water would be a B shot, and a nine-iron back to the fairway would be a C shot. Before you make a decision as to which you'll attempt, relate how you are playing *right now* (not how you hope to be playing in two years), to the difficulty factor combined with the potential penalty factor.

This is what the pros call percentage golf. Most of the time they'll play either the B shot or the C shot. One of the chief reasons 100-plus shooters aren't minus-90 shooters is that most of the time they try to play the A shot.

Most of the disaster holes that occur in professional tournament golf are products of the mind, not the muscles. Generally they begin with either a poor shot or an unlucky bounce placing the golfer in some

If you really are committed to reducing your score, do some work on your short game.

degree of trouble. Invariably he tries to do too much with the recovery, either out of anger and frustration or an over-ambitious assessment of his own capabilities in his eagerness not to give away a stroke. By compounding the error he ends up giving away a hatful of strokes.

High handicappers do this sort of thing continually, and I have to believe one of the reasons is that they simply don't know, beyond very broad parameters, what it is possible to do with a golf club and ball—and what it is not possible to do. Continually in pro-ams I see amateurs attempt shots that I would never even consider, simply because I know they are mechanically impossible. Conceivably the golfer trying to hit a three iron out of four inches of wet rough, or loft a three wood over a tree from a severe downhill lie, simply doesn't know that it flat can't be done.

If you suspect that this might be a reason why you seem to run up a disaster every time you leave the fairway, here's a tip that will definitely help you while you're learning more about the game's mechanical cause-and-effect factors.

Before you grab a club from the bag, go and actually put yourself in position over the ball; study how it lies. You'll find that setting up as though to play the shot, but without a stick in your hand, gives you a pretty clear instinctual picture of its difficulty factor. Let yourself be governed by that. The more difficult any shot "feels" to you instinctually, the more difficult it undoubtedly is. Play accordingly and you'll have far fewer disasters.

Most of my career I've played with a fade—a very slight left-to-right shot. If you're a 100-shooter, it's a cast-iron certainty that most of the golf you've played has been with a slice—a much bigger version of my "shape."

There is no doubt that you would have a better chance of breaking 90 if you could reduce either the amount your long shots curve to the right or, better yet, learn how to curve them to the left. To do so, you would probably need some instruction, and most definitely you would need more than a little practice. If neither of those measures is appealing, then at least decide to accept what you have and learn how to play with it.

For example, if you now slice the ball most of the time, *don't* aim for the middle of the fairway or green in the hope that "this time" you'll hit it straight. You won't, because miracles don't happen in golf. What you'll do most of the time, by aiming for the center of the course, is slice the ball into trouble on the right. So compensate for your error instead of fighting it. Simply aim left on all long shots and let the ball curve back onto the mown playing surfaces. That way you've got the entire width of the fairway or green at your disposal. This is not an elegant way to play golf, of course, but if you're more interested in scores than aesthetics, it sure beats continually hacking out of all that tall timber off to starboard.

If you're that very rare individual—the 100-shooter who habitually hooks the ball—then obviously you reverse the procedure, aiming down the right-hand side and letting the ball curve back to the left.

This type of strategy is what the pros call "going with the A to B shot." Every golfer finds it easier to curve the ball one way or the other. Better players will almost always go with their "natural" shape whenever they absolutely must get the ball from point A to point B under heavy pressure.

It's been said before a million times, but it's got to be said again. If you really are committed to reducing your score, but don't have whatever it would take to remodel your full-shot swing, then do some work on your short game—the shots to and around and on the green.

I spend a lot of fruitful time simply dropping and playing balls at random around my backyard putting green. It's a pleasantly challenging way to spend a quiet after-dinner hour on a summer evening, either in your own backyard or on an empty golf course.

Start by repeating, say, the same simple chip shot until you begin to "muscle-memorize" a basic stroking pattern. Do the same with short pitch shots; then move into a sand trap and stay there until you are able to get every ball at least out and onto the green. Do this fairly regularly and you'll enjoy an immediate score reduction, not only because of your improved physical skills, but through the reduction of pressure on your long game that short-game confidence breeds.

From what I see in pro-ams, there are three areas in particular where even slight short-game improvement would bring a lot of amateurs immediately into the 80s.

Bunkers are where I'd first put most of my high-handicap partners to work. The reason they so frequently fail to get out is that simply being in sand paralyzes them with fear. One hour of just dropping the club through the sand under the ball would conquer that terror forever.

Learning that roll is both easier to execute and judge than flight, would be second on the curriculum. Trying to loft rather than run every just-off-the-green shot is a standard mistake among high handicappers.

Finally, I'd suggest a couple of long-putt practice sessions, first to develop stroking fluidity, but primarily to teach that power—distance—is much more the critical factor than direction on most long putts. Sheer instinct will generally take care of direction, whereas the amount of force you are going to impart to the ball has to be very finely judged and "felt" mentally *before* you move the club.

In the final analysis, however, trying in golf comes down to the same thing as in every other facet of life, which is desire. If you want to break 90 badly enough, you'll keep on trying, and one day it will happen. And then, of course, you'll want to break 80, and then 70. . . . Which, in a nutshell, is what makes golf the great game that it is. ∎

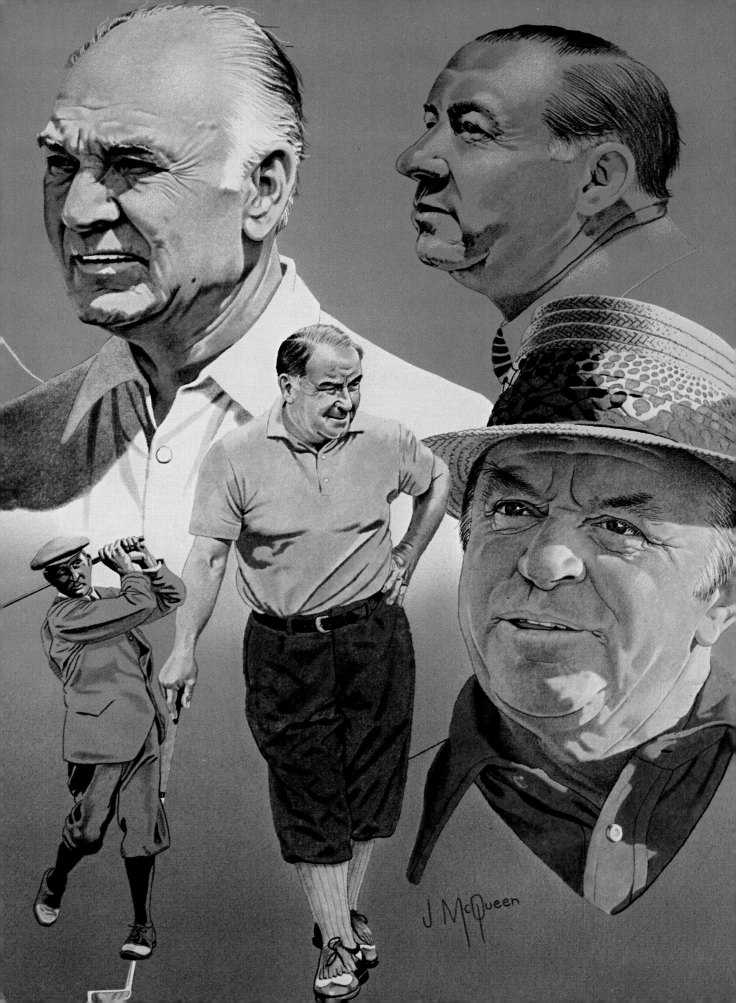

J. McQueen

Inner Game 6:

Superstar Psychoanalysis – How to Use the Mind to Win

I've tried so far in this series to give you an insight into the mental factors behind my own golf game. To conclude the series I think it would be interesting— and instructive—to look into the personalities and mental characteristics of the great golfers. I'm certainly no historian or psychologist, but I've always enjoyed studying and learning from the old champions, and inevitably have formed impressions about the great modern players I've enjoyed competing against.

I suppose the first true superstar of golf, the first to win national opens on both sides of the Atlantic, was Harry Vardon. From all I've read and heard about Vardon, his greatest assets were his effortlessness and accuracy from tee to green—the records indicate that when healthy he never lost a tournament through tiredness, and that he could knock a brassie within 15 feet of the pin seven times out of 10.

Even though those results derive from a marvelous swing, they also seem to me to be rooted in a certain temperamental or mental approach to the game. By all accounts Vardon was a placid individual—the kind of fellow, like Julius Boros in more recent years, who either by nature or self-discipline could remain pretty

Hagen: "I never played a perfect 18 holes. There is no such thing."

much at peace with himself whatever was happening to him on the golf course.

I'm not advocating apathy, but I know from my own experience that one of the worst mistakes you can make in golf is trying to *force* the game. Patience is essential. You are going to have ups and downs, good breaks and bad breaks, successful days and unsuccessful days.

A certain amount of emotional stability is also the strongest defense against the two most common fears in golf—fear of failing and fear of winning. Golf was Vardon's livelihood, and also no doubt his joy, but I doubt very much from what I've learned of him if tournament golf was ever *life itself* to him. Win or lose, you get the impression that to him there was always another day, another tournament. Nothing will keep a man's muscles looser and his swing more "peaceful" than that kind of attitude.

Hagen realistic about a bad shot
Walter Hagen was the first great American-born professional and, although just about the polar opposite of Vardon in personality, he also possessed great golfing equanimity. If one believes all one reads and hears about Hagen, he was just about the least blessed champion ever in terms of swing technique. Where he excelled was in cheerfully accepting his shotmaking limitations and overcoming them with a marvelous short game, an intense competitive spirit, and unshakable self-confidence.

The essence of the man—and the mental attitude that made Hagen a champion—is contained in one of his best-known quotes: "I've never played a perfect 18 holes. There is no such thing. I expect to make at least seven mistakes a round. Therefore, when I make a bad shot, I don't worry about it. It's just one of the seven." His realism freed the mind to move on positively to the next shot, the next day, the next tournament.

Hagen offers another lesson in his dedication to living life to its fullest off the golf course. Once he left the course, he removed himself mentally from golf as far as he possibly could, which I'm sure was the key to his sustaining freshness and enthusiasm for the game. Too much of anything breeds staleness in most people, and Hagen never fell into that trap.

Sarazen didn't hide his competitiveness
Gene Sarazen, who rivaled Hagen as the world's top professional in the '20s and '30s, was a very different personality, but one thing Hagen and Sarazen—and every other great golfer—had in common is a highly developed competitive drive. Many competitive people take pains to hide this aspect of their nature because of the adverse affect aggressiveness can have on their popularity when it's blatantly exposed.

Particularly in his youth, Sarazen not only did not

bother to hide his competitiveness, but let it work for him as a psychological weapon. The great golf writer O. B. Keeler perfectly described this characteristic of Sarazen when he wrote: "When Gene takes the field against any golfer, or any array of golfers, the only question in his mind is, in the first instance, how many holes will it take him to beat his man, and, in the second, by what margin is he going to finish in front.'

The golfer probably closest to Sarazen in this respect today is Hale Irwin. Hale simply cannot help showing his intense competitiveness, his will to win, in his facial expressions and general mannerisms, and sometimes, when the fires burn particularly strong, even in his conversation. But whether he or she shows it or not, every champion is an extremely competitive animal—a person to whom winning is a good part of what life's all about. Even though I may not show it much in public, it's there in my own case not only in golf but in any activity that involves a contest.

Jones learned to control his inner turmoil
Bobby Jones rarely displayed his competitiveness in his mature years, but it would have been impossible for him to have compiled his wonderful record without a powerful competitive drive. Where Jones excelled probably more than any other golfer, once he grew up, was in never letting competitiveness cause him to lose control of his emotions.

Irrational and impetuous action and general loss of perspective, born of anger and frustration, are great dangers for the highly competitive person when things aren't going well. Jones' fine intellect and sense of values enabled him to exert a high degree of self-discipline at such times. He tried his utmost to win every time he teed up, but if he failed he could quiet his emotional turmoil and accept failure gracefully on the outside, by recognizing that no one can win all the time and that there would be plenty more opportunities.

I don't think there can be much doubt that some people are inherently more physically gifted for golf than others. Bob Jones, for example, seemed to combine strength and suppleness in an ideal blend. So, probably more than any other great golfer, does Sam Snead. Both were also naturally blessed with great mind/muscle or hand/eye coordination, which was probably the source of their great tempo and rhythm. I was also blessed with excellent inherent coordination, and am also gifted with strong legs, maybe the single biggest natural asset a golfer can have. But, there have been quite a number of great players who did not appear to start out with any special physical gifts, and I think collectively they offer one extremely pertinent mental example.

Among them, Ben Hogan, Henry Cotton, Bobby Locke, Cary Middecoff, Gary Player and Lee Trevino have won 34 major championships. Yet none of these fellows was particularly gifted for golf when he first

It is the mind much more than the method that makes a golf champion.

began to play the game, and I think each would confirm that his eventual great talents came much more from training, study and sweat-provoking effort than from the raw materials he possessed at the outset.

If that's true, then it's the best example I can think of to highlight the one quality above all others that makes a champion, at golf or anything else. That one indispensable quality is desire. Desire to excel is the motivator, the ultimate driving force.

Desire drove Hogan to be a perfectionist

What the champions and potential champions recognize, that the handicap player frequently doesn't, is that success in shotmaking ultimately doesn't come from building a swing that will produce great shots. Even Ben Hogan, the greatest perfectionist in golfing history, admits that he never played more than six shots exactly as he planned in any one round, and that's certainly as many as I can generally hope for. The goal is not perfection but a continual narrowing of the margin between a player's best and worst shots through identification of and adherence to the techniques that work best for the individual.

Once a basically effective method has been developed, the ongoing effort of the champion is to improve within his own established pattern—*to make the best of what he's got.*

It is often said, and I'm sure it's true, that it is the mind much more than the method that makes a golf champion, and each of the players we've just mentioned bears this out. Ben Hogan is famous for having practiced probably more than any other great player, and that reflects huge amounts of dedication and self-discipline. The same is true of those other two intense practicers, Henry Cotton and Gary Player. Both of them, not being inherently powerful, disciplined themselves with rigorous physical conditioning programs and generally spartan life styles on top of their back-breaking golfing regimens. You can miss an awful lot in life when you dedicate yourself that totally to one activity, but for many who want to be champions it is the only way to get there.

Perfectionism can be a particularly tough characteristic for a golfer to live with. Cary Middlecoff was one of golf's great perfectionists, and perhaps it was this trait as much as back trouble that eventually led him to take the game easier. Fortunately, thus far I've been able to temper my own tendency to want to do things as well as possible with a certain amount of fatalism when they don't work out. But this temperamental characteristic is definitely a major driving force in my life. Where it has helped particularly in golf is in making me always try to identify the perfect shot in my mind before I step up to the ball. The fatalism—or maybe realism is a better word—comes into play when I then fail to execute it, which is most of the time. But the desire for perfection, or at least to do some-thing as well as it possibly can be done, is in my case unquestionably a stimulus to keep on playing and trying to improve at golf.

Snead plays for fun—and never gets stale

I mentioned Sam Snead as having a lot of natural physical talent for golf. Where Sam excels mentally is in always being able to enjoy the game—in playing it for fun as much as for a living. Sam certainly wouldn't be playing tournaments in his 60s if this weren't true, and I think it's maybe the main reason he has been able to play so well so long.

It is difficult to excel at something you don't enjoy. To keep myself enjoying the game, I like to get completely away from it at times. After a few days or weeks of other activities I'm always eager just to get out and play golf simply for the sake of playing. Sam, of course, has been unusual in that he could play virtually every day without ever getting stale, which is not true of most champions.

Palmer's willpower his greatest quality

Of all the mental qualities we've discussed here, can any one be singled out as the primary source of golfing excellence? Many ingredients are necessary to play great golf, but if I had to pick one mental characteristic above all others that have produced champions I think it would probably be willpower: the will to achieve, to excel, to be the best, to win. And the fellow I'd choose to exemplify this quality is my old sparring partner, Arnold Palmer.

Arnold has a great many good qualities, but the one that struck me most whenever we played together when he was at his peak was the strength of will with which he attacked the game. You could see it in the aggressiveness of his long shots, in his mannerisms, in the way he carried himself on the course. But you could sense it most—actually feel it coming from him in waves—on the greens.

Arnie had a fabulous touch and a fine if highly individualistic putting technique, but it wasn't just these that got the ball in the hole time and again from 30 or 40 feet, or rammed it against the back of the can after he'd putted four or five feet past on the first try. More than anything else you got the feeling that he actually *willed* the ball into the hole.

An opponent's intellect told him that nobody can put the ball on the green from the middle of a forest and then hole it from 60 feet by virtue of sheer will-power alone, but the emotional feeling that Arnold did just that was definitely one of the factors that made him so tough to beat.

Few champions have shown this quality as obviously as Arnie, but it has been there in all of them. In fact, the more I think about it, the more I'm inclined to believe that willpower is the factor that most separates the great from the good. ■

Part II
Playing Lessons

Golf is You Against Yourself

1. Golf isn't just ball control—knowing where and how to hit the ball and then being capable of doing it. In the final analysis golf is self-control—man against himself. You've got to whip yourself before you can whip any golf course. If you can't accept that—and keep working at it—you'll never be a winner.

2. Self-control demands self-honesty above all else. Learn to fight emotionalism with realism. Accept first and foremost the cold fact that every shot you hit, good or bad, is the product of only one person: YOU. Accept, secondly, that you rarely if ever will play or score quite as well as you think you can and should. I never have. Accept, thirdly, that golf by its nature involves a high degree of luck, but the luck always evens out. Finally, recognize and accept your own shot-making limitations: know what you *definitely* can do with the ball, what you *might* be able to do with it, and what you definitely *cannot* do with it. Play accordingly.

3. Being realistic doesn't mean being pessimi Having a poorer record in the U.S. Open than in the other major championships doesn't make me think I can't win each new year's Open. It's an incentive to extra effort. A winning attitude is essential every time you te it up, and a winning attitude demands two things: living in the *present,* not the past or future, and *believing that you are the best* at your own level of competition. If a poor qualifying score has placed you in the second flight of the club championship when you thin you should rightfully be in the first, don't let what's behind you destroy what's ahead of yo Build faith in yourself by winning the second flight this time as a stepping stone to winning the championship flight *next* time.

4. Golf's leisureliness and friendliness make concentration a tough self-disciplinary challenge for many players. Some seem unable ever to get their minds fully on the job. My approach is to relax fully between shots by letting my mind roam where it will, then snap back to the task at hand by forming a very specific mental visualization of the perfect shot for the particular situation I'm faced with. Once I've locked that picture in place, I keep my mind from wandering by focusing on one or at most two specific swing thoughts related to the execution of the shot I've planned.

J McQueen

5. Indecisiveness can result from fear, but it also can result from nothing more than muddled thinking—a prime example of poor self-discipline. The worst personal example I can recall, which left a permanent lesson, came in the 1963 U.S. Open at Brookline. I should have gone in charged up as defending champion, but actually I was full of the worst kind of indecision. I didn't know whether I wanted to hit the ball from right to left as I had been doing because of a minor hip ailment, or from left to right as I basically prefer and as the course seemed to require. The result was 76-77 and a humiliating departure after 36 holes. I've never since played a tournament without deciding which basic shot shape I intend to use.

6. I earned my first big check as a pro and learned a lot about golf's toughest self-disciplinary challenge of all in the 1962 Thunderbird Classic in New Jersey. I was close to the leaders after 36 holes, but I started Round Three with three three-putts and a tee shot under a bush on the fourth hole. If I'd had anything better to do, I might have quit right there. The urge was certainly strong. Instead, I knocked the ball out of the bush, knocked it on and knocked it in. I got such a lift I birdied 10 of the last 14 holes for a 65 and second place. The moral? Keep trying, keep trucking, *whatever* happens. One good shot can turn everything around. No one wins or loses at golf until the last putt is holed.

thunderbird CLASSIC

HOLES	1	2	3	4	5	6	7	8	9	OUT	10	11	12	13	14	15	16	17	18	IN	TOTAL
YARDS	375	360	210	425	525	425	555	210	450	3535	435	530	440	350	365	190	410	230	600	3550	7085
PAR	4	4	3	4	5	4	5	3	4	36	4	5	4	4	3	3	4	3	5	36	72
	5	5	4																	30	65

Jack Nicklaus

Your Most Important Shot in a Round of Golf

1. What's the most important shot in a round of golf? Your longest drive? Your closest approach? The "impossible" recovery shot you fluked in for a birdie? Your winning putt? Not in my book. If any one shot is more important than any other—which is arguable—then it's the same shot every time: *the opening drive.* Obviously I give every golf shot maximum effort (even on the practice tee), but that opening blow always gets 100-percent-*plus,* for the simple reason it so often sets the mood for the entire round. Hit it well and confidence surges. Hit it poorly and sour thoughts immediately begin to flood the psyche. They may go away if you play the next shot well, but too often you won't because doubt has already been planted. So try your darndest for a strong opener.

2. The big killer on the first tee—for me as much as for you—is tension, both physical and mental. A productive warm-up session will help to free both the mind and the muscles. A few deep breaths as you walk onto the tee and a few slow and easy practice swings once you get there also will help. For me, the ultimate answer to first-tee stress is *deliberation.* I'm especially tense on a big occasion, such as the 1977 British Open at Turnberry (first hole shown here). In your case, just the inevitable first-tee gallery will often add pressure to an already tight situation. Either way, there's an involuntary urge to hurry—to shorten the agony. I never hit any golf shot until I'm ready, but on the first one I always make a conscious effort to be *extra* deliberate, first in planning the shot, then in setup, and finally in swing tempo.

3. You will not achieve success whenever you lack confidence in the club in your hand. If you can't play a driver—and very few high handicappers can, especially first thing in the round—then forget both distance and what you suspect your pals may think about your manhood. Use the longest club in which you have confidence and *get the ball in play,* even if it's only a 4-iron. A solid first shot, even if it's a short one, generally will set up at worst a bogey and you may even get a par. A disaster on the first hole usually will set up a day of frustration.

SLOW

NO. 1
425 YD
PAR

J McQueen

4. It's human nature to save the big effort until last. Maybe that's OK in a sport like boxing, but in golf it's extremely poor strategy. There are 18 holes in a round of golf and often more in a tournament, and *every one counts equally.* So don't be a lazy player—don't live in the future by letting yourself "cruise" at the beginning in the hope or belief that you can storm at the end. The odds generally are that you'll play worse the farther you go through sheer fatigue, plus, if you're in contention, mounting pressure. So give it your best from the word go—try your utmost *now.* In stroke play the better you play earlier, the greater your confidence and the greater the cushion you build against a bad bounce or swing hitch. In match play think in terms of going 1 up on the first hole, 2 up on the second, 3 up on the third, and so on until you're 10 up on the 10th green and shaking hands. It will rarely happen that way, of course, but it's a great attitude to have on the first tee.

5. Anger is Golfing Enemy No. 1. The most stupid example that I see among amateurs is the guy who gets so enraged over bad shots that he loses balls simply by not watching and marking where they go. The most common example I see on tour is the vicious circle born of a person's inability to recognize and accept his own fallibility and/or the fact that golf is not 100 percent fair. Step One in this unappealing process is getting angry at some external element like the condition of the course or the behavior of the gallery as an excuse for your own mistake or an unlucky bounce. Step Two is getting angrier still in response to your fear about coping with the problem. Step Three is getting more angry at the even worse situation you create as a result of your diminishing control. Step Four is getting angrier yet at the course or crowd, until you just flat quit or drift into slaphappy despondency.

6. I've lost at least some of my cool a few times, but rarely all of it because I was fortunate to recognize two things about golf at a very early age. One is that I'm always going to make mistakes. The other is that overcoming both your own errors and bad bounces is just as much a part of the game's challenge as trying to hit perfect shots. But that's philosophy and easily forgotten in the heat of the moment, so let me offer a *specific* counter to that feeling of rising blood pressure. When you hit a terrible shot or get a criminally bad break, put it out of your mind by immediately forcing yourself to think hard about your *next* shot. Picture as fast and clearly as you can what you *now* must try to do with the ball and how you're going to do it. Make that a mental habit and you'll be surprised how calmly you can play this inherently irritating game—and how much better you can recover from its slings and arrows.

How to Learn by Watching and Asking

1. Playing golf strategically demands the ability to fit your shots to a wide variety of playing conditions. I haven't *fundamentally* changed my golf swing since I was 13 years old, but I've never stopped trying to increase my *versatility* as a shotmaker. Pride has never stopped me from seeking help in this area. Much of the knowledge I possess I've cribbed from other tour players, both by watching and asking. You can—and should—do the same whenever you get the chance to play with good golfers.

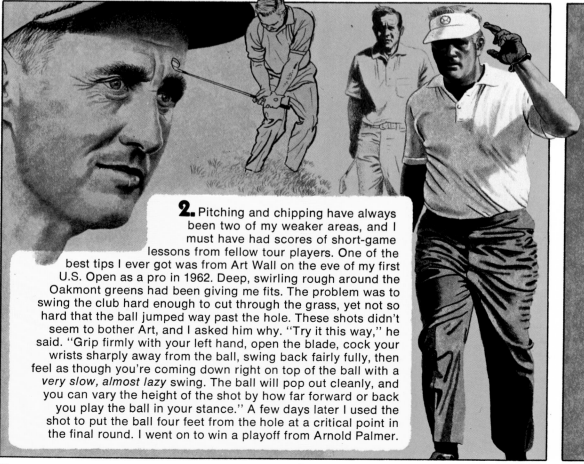

2. Pitching and chipping have always been two of my weaker areas, and I must have had scores of short-game lessons from fellow tour players. One of the best tips I ever got was from Art Wall on the eve of my first U.S. Open as a pro in 1962. Deep, swirling rough around the Oakmont greens had been giving me fits. The problem was to swing the club hard enough to cut through the grass, yet not so hard that the ball jumped way past the hole. These shots didn't seem to bother Art, and I asked him why. "Try it this way," he said. "Grip firmly with your left hand, open the blade, cock your wrists sharply away from the ball, swing back fairly fully, then feel as though you're coming down right on top of the ball with a *very slow, almost lazy* swing. The ball will pop out cleanly, and you can vary the height of the shot by how far forward or back you play the ball in your stance." A few days later I used the shot to put the ball four feet from the hole at a critical point in the final round. I went on to win a playoff from Arnold Palmer.

3. Most people who love golf are like Art—eager to help another person play better, even when they might end up losing to the pupil (I once saw two tournament leaders practicing for the final round and giving each other tips!). I never have hesitated to seek help. In fact, there was a period when Deane Beman and Gary Player, my longtime putting and sand teachers, almost had to hide from me during practice sessions to get time for their own games.

4. I'm not nearly as rabid a lesson-taker as Gary—he's the ultimate, especially in the area of fundamentals. But I'll listen to anyone whose knowledge I respect or who knows my game, especially when I'm playing poorly and haven't been able to figure out why. My wife Barbara is no Bob Toski, but she's always been my No. 1 fault-spotter simply because she knows my game so well. I couldn't begin to count the number of times a sign or word from her about my head movement, for example, has set my putting straight. If your wife knows golf, and especially your golf, invite her opinion when things aren't going well. Ask one of the guys you play with regularly what he thinks. Because you can't see yourself, it's often the basic things you take for granted that go wrong. Setup alignment requires constant checking, for instance. Golfers rarely will risk imposing by volunteering information, but when they're asked, the knowledgeable ones often will give you just the word or thought that pinpoints the flaw.

5. If you're a really serious golfer, consider investing in a movie camera as a self-teaching aid. Eleven years ago I won my third Masters, in a playoff, as a result of seeing on a TV replay what caused me to miss a three-foot putt on the 71st hole of regulation play. That led eventually to my purchasing a home video-recorder. I ask friends to tape the telecasts of tournaments where I'm likely to be on camera. When I've played poorly, watching the reruns has been the first item on my agenda when I get home—in the middle of the night on a couple of occasions. If you know what you *should* be doing, there's nothing like being able to see yourself to find out why you're not doing it.

6. If you're a good golfer going through a long lean spell, or a poor player who really hungers to get better, find yourself a golf professional who'll take enough interest in you to get to know your game thoroughly, then go see him on a *regular* basis. My indebtedness to my teacher, Jack Grout, isn't just for what he taught me as a kid, but for the pain he's been able to save me on an ongoing basis. Having a man like Grout in the wings has meant that I could get help in the *early stages* of a problem, rather than wait until it's become a game-wrecker. I don't run to him every time I miss a fairway, because if golf demands anything it's self-knowledge and self-reliance. But I do go to Jack as soon as I recognize I have a problem that is going to be tough for me to work out. That's saved me untold frustration. If you take the game seriously, get your pride out of the way and get yourself a friendly teacher. Remember, whatever it may feel like, you can't see yourself swing at a golf ball.

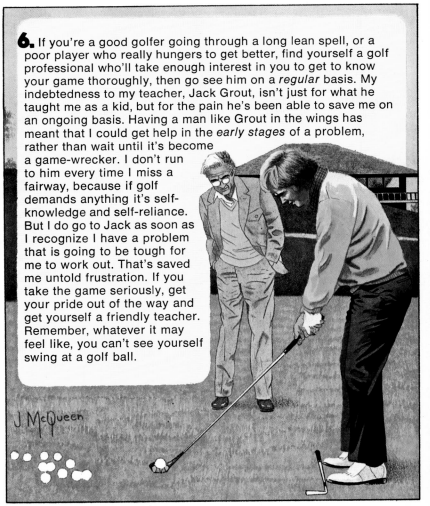

J. McQueen

How to Prepare for a Tournament

1. I learned a lot about preparation the hard way in my first overseas tournament as a pro, a 72-hole event at the very rugged Hillside links next door to Royal Birkdale in England. I'd committed way in advance, then been so busy I could fly over only two days ahead of time. I went straight from Texas heat and the American-size ball through a six-hour time change to bitter cold and dampness and the smaller British ball—plus I didn't have anywhere near enough time to learn the course. The result was 79-71-70-78—298, a lot of embarrassment and a lasting lesson.

What the experience brought home to me is that preparation—advance thinking and planning—is crucial. You can't plan ahead if you don't know what lies ahead, which is ample reason for playing practice rounds prior to any important contest. My preparation starts weeks ahead of any big event, with three basic questions I ask myself about the golf course. First, is it most susceptible to a fade or a draw? Second, how big a factor will distance be? Third, can I generally gamble or must I usually play safe?

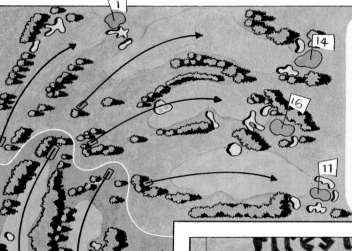

2. Question one will be answered primarily by the shape of the holes related to the anticipated ground and weather conditions. For example, the popular tournament site, Pebble Beach (top left), has a great many left-to-right holes which, combined with the usually firm turf, definitely favor a fade. Augusta National, on the other hand, moves predominantly from right to left, especially from the tees (bottom left). Generally for the Masters I have settled on a draw off the tee, with a readiness to play a high fade to the greens on a number of the longer holes. Having made that decision, in practice I'll be working well ahead of time on the swing pattern that produces the ball flight I've selected.

HOLE	1	2	3	4	5	6	7	8	9	OUT	10	11	12	13	14	15	16	17	18
YARDS	400	500	450	465	230	465	225	450	465	3650	405	365	180	460	410	230	625	390	46
	4	5	4				4		4	35	4	4	3	4	4	3	5	4	2

3. Question two—the distance factor—will be answered primarily by the length of the course and the anticipated texture of its turf. For example, Firestone is both long—it has five par 4s over 460 yards and three par 3s over 225—and usually also very lush. Those considerations obviously make distance the top priority. Accordingly, I work up to this type of course by switching drives with my boys when we play at home to provide practice on long shots to the greens. You can achieve the same effect by reversing your tee and approach shots—driving, say, with the 5-iron, *then* hitting the 3-wood or a long iron to the green. Immediately after playing Firestone one year, I shifted to medium- and short-iron work in my practice to prepare for the Ryder Cup matches at Royal Lytham in England, where precision was sure to be more important than power.

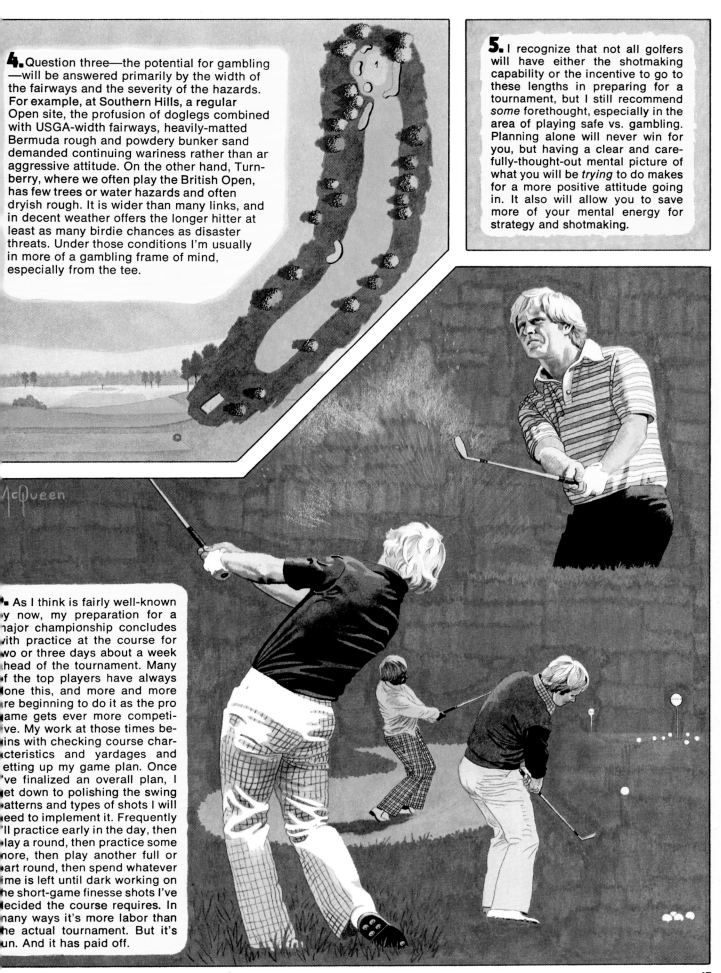

4. Question three—the potential for gambling—will be answered primarily by the width of the fairways and the severity of the hazards. For example, at Southern Hills, a regular Open site, the profusion of doglegs combined with USGA-width fairways, heavily-matted Bermuda rough and powdery bunker sand demanded continuing wariness rather than an aggressive attitude. On the other hand, Turnberry, where we often play the British Open, has few trees or water hazards and often dryish rough. It is wider than many links, and in decent weather offers the longer hitter at least as many birdie chances as disaster threats. Under those conditions I'm usually in more of a gambling frame of mind, especially from the tee.

5. I recognize that not all golfers will have either the shotmaking capability or the incentive to go to these lengths in preparing for a tournament, but I still recommend *some* forethought, especially in the area of playing safe vs. gambling. Planning alone will never win for you, but having a clear and carefully-thought-out mental picture of what you will be *trying* to do makes for a more positive attitude going in. It also will allow you to save more of your mental energy for strategy and shotmaking.

As I think is fairly well-known by now, my preparation for a major championship concludes with practice at the course for two or three days about a week ahead of the tournament. Many of the top players have always done this, and more and more are beginning to do it as the pro game gets ever more competitive. My work at those times begins with checking course characteristics and yardages and setting up my game plan. Once I've finalized an overall plan, I get down to polishing the swing patterns and types of shots I will need to implement it. Frequently I'll practice early in the day, then play a round, then practice some more, then play another full or part round, then spend whatever time is left until dark working on the short-game finesse shots I've decided the course requires. In many ways it's more labor than the actual tournament. But it's fun. And it has paid off.

Taking the Guesswork Out of Judging Distance

1. Most golfers underclub approach shots most of the time. One reason is pure ego—thinking you are longer than you really are. A second reason is lack of realism—believing you'll hit every shot 100 percent solidly even though no one ever has. A third reason is a failure to notice that there generally is more trouble in front of and to the sides of greens than beyond them. But the big reason is neglect of a basic preplanning necessity: *knowing the distance from your ball to the green.*

2. Deane Beman, now PGA Tour Commissioner, introduced me to actually measuring approach-shot yardages while we were practicing for the 1961 U.S. Amateur at Pebble Beach. I used it in actual play, was under par in every match, won the championship, realized what tremendous help it gave me, and I have paced off every course on which I've competed ever since.

3. Knowing rather than guessing the distance of any given approach shot is a tremendous aid to club selection. That alone makes measuring well worth the effort, but the benefits go much deeper. Confidence and concentration are ultimate keys to golfing success, and if there is any doubt in your mind about the distance, it is bound to undermine them. The uncertainty may be subconscious, but that doesn't make it any less costly. Knowing the yardage enables you to focus far more positively on shot execution.

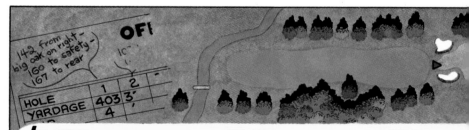

4. My measuring technique is simple. During practice I first identify a permanent object that is a few yards short of where my drive normally would finish: a mature tree, the tip of a bunker, the corner of a house, a sprinkler head. From there I pace out the distance in one-yard steps to the front and rear edges of the green. If a trap or water hazard eats deeply into the front of a green, I also pace the distance to the "safety" zone. I note all these factors on scorecards, which I keep and file for future reference (I now have some 600 from all around the world). Thus armed, it becomes a simple matter in tournament play to calculate the distance of any approach shot by pacing off the difference between my fixed marker and where my drive has finished, then assessing the pin position in relation to the depth of the green and doing a little math. Angelo, my caddie, also goes through the same process and we compare notes for a double check. I do this on all shots over 50 or 60 yards. On shorter shots, feel is more critical than precise yardage.

NO. 7
PAR 3
156 YDS

5. Playing as much golf as I do, I keep pretty current on how far I normally hit the ball with each club. The best way to determine your distances if you don't play a lot of golf is to pace them off periodically on a practice range. If that's impractical or too much bother, then keep a reckoning of your performance on par-3 holes. Assuming the card yardages are accurate and you relate them correctly to tee-marker positions, the par 3s can give you a helpful picture of your distance capability with most clubs in the bag. Also, 150-yard markers offer a similar opportunity. Whatever method you choose, don't be surprised if you find you're a shorter hitter than you thought you were—and *use* that lesson in your club selection from now on.

Conditions influence clubbing, but even in extreme circumstances I find knowing my distances immensely valuable. In the 66 British Open at Muirfield I knew I had to make birdie on the 8-yard 71st hole to have a real chance of winning. My 3-iron wnwind tee shot (I took an iron to avoid running through the gleg) left me 238 yards from the center of the green. Normally th the U.S.-size ball that would call for a 1-iron, but condins there were very different. Here's how I worked out the ot that won me my first British Open: "One club less for the all ball, one club less for the run I'll get landing short of the en on this firm fairway, one and a half clubs less for the folwing wind, and a half club less for the extra distance the renalin flow is giving me. That's a 5-iron." I put the ball 16 feet m the flag. Without the precise yardage as a base for calcuing the shot, I probably would have put it way over the green.

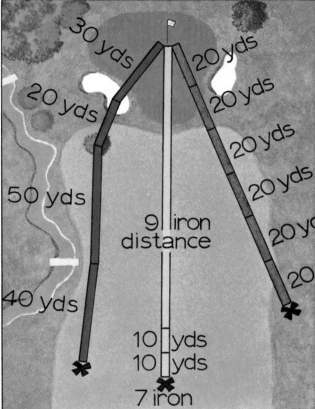

30 yds
20 yds
20 yds
20 yds
20 yds
20 yds
20 yds
20 y
20
50 yds
40 yds
9 iron distance
10 yds
10 yds
7 iron

7. If pacing off courses is too much for you, there are a number of other proven ways to figure distance. One is to estimate by increments, picturing first a short segment of distance, then adding comparable chunks until your eyes reach the flag. A little experiment will tell you what size segment you can picture most effectively—I've usually done best with 20- or 50-yard progressions. Or you can estimate from landmark to landmark: "Sixty yards from here to that tree, 90 from the tree to that bunker, 25 from the bunker to the flag." Another way is to identify a point that is wedge or 9-iron distance from the green, then go up club by club for each 10-yard increment as your eyes work back to your ball position. Pick one of these techniques and try it over your next 10 rounds. I'd almost bet it will cut a few shots off your score.

Getting Prepared to Play Your Best

1. Being prepared to play golf starts way ahead of getting up early enough to hit a few warm-up shots on tournament mornings. It involves making the game as easy as you possibly can by getting yourself totally ready to play at your best long before you actually draw a club from the bag. A fellow I played with a few weeks ago in a pro-am dramatizes the point. He began by borrowing a tee and ended up getting saturated because he brought no rain gear or umbrella. In between he had to ask distances on most holes for want of a scorecard. He eliminated himself from a couple of holes by unwittingly breaking rules. Looking for some excuse for his horrible play, he asked me after the round to check out his clubs, which I'd have been happy to do if I could have held on to them—the grips were slicker than a bare metal shaft. Obviously, that amount of discombobulation in one golfer is unusual, but these and other examples of disorganization seem to be fairly common in the amateur game.

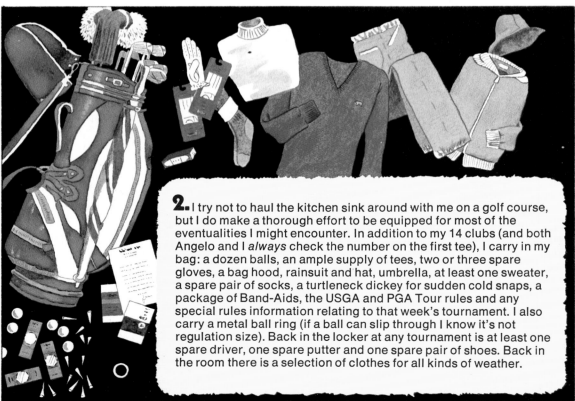

2. I try not to haul the kitchen sink around with me on a golf course, but I do make a thorough effort to be equipped for most of the eventualities I might encounter. In addition to my 14 clubs (and both Angelo and I *always* check the number on the first tee), I carry in my bag: a dozen balls, an ample supply of tees, two or three spare gloves, a bag hood, rainsuit and hat, umbrella, at least one sweater, a spare pair of socks, a turtleneck dickey for sudden cold snaps, a package of Band-Aids, the USGA and PGA Tour rules and any special rules information relating to that week's tournament. I also carry a metal ball ring (if a ball can slip through I know it's not regulation size). Back in the locker at any tournament is at least one spare driver, one spare putter and one spare pair of shoes. Back in the room there is a selection of clothes for all kinds of weather.

3. When it comes to rules, I'm certainly not an expert, but I *have* studied them sufficiently to know at least their basic provisions, especially in regard to the penalties they exact and the relief they permit. Over the years I've come to realize that the rules, complex as they may seem, are essential to sustaining the spirit of equity and sportsmanship that makes golf such a uniquely great game. Once you accept their basic tenets, they can help you as much as they can hurt you.

4. I got my first and sharpest lesson in the rules in the 1960 U.S. Open at Cherry Hills. Age 20 and still an amateur—and paired with Ben Hogan—I somehow had a one-shot lead over a tight pack of great names with only six holes to play. I hit an excellent 3-wood tee shot followed by a 9-iron 12 feet from the pin at the 385-yard 67th hole. All of a sudden it dawned on me exactly where I was and what I had a chance of doing. I hit my first putt 18 inches past the hole, then made possibly the worst mistake of my entire golfing career. Directly on my line was an old, improperly-repaired ball mark. In my excitement I became concerned and confused over what I could do about it—I was even too scared to ask an official for advice. So I went ahead and hit the putt and it caught the ball mark and spun out of the hole. I three-putted the next green and missed an easy five-foot birdie putt on the 70th hole to finish second, two shots back of Arnold Palmer. The rule about ball marks on greens is crystal clear and absolutely in the golfer's favor: you can repair them, any time, any place.

HOGAN
NICKLAL

J McQueen

5. There isn't space here to go into all the situations in which you can obtain relief under the rules, but here's just one small example that may tempt you into a closer familiarity with them (a copy of the rules is available for 50 cents from the USGA, Far Hills, N.J. 07931). You probably already know that you don't have to play from a puddle in the fairway, but do you also know that the "casual water" rule also gives you penalty-free relief from temporary water accumulations in both hazards and rough? You also can *clean* the ball—often a big break in sloppy conditions—when you lift it to drop clear of casual water, as you can in at least five other lifting and dropping situations. To discover what those are, read Rule 23. And while you have the book in hand, also read Rule 12 about playing a provisional ball from the tee in match play—it might save you some stress and embarrassment against a rules-respecting opponent.

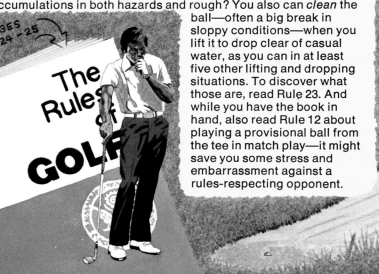

6. When it comes to the negative aspects of the rules—the penalties—those that are always uppermost in my mind concern a ball seemingly at rest moving after I've addressed it but before I've hit it (basically, Rules 25, 27, 31, 33 and 35). They make me very cautious about moving loose impediments and/or soling my club if I sense the slightest instability in the ball—even on the putting green. But even here it's not all gloom and despondency, *provided* you really understand what the rules say. I've seen a lot of players suffer penalties over the years through failure to take safeguards that would be automatic if they had known the rules. I've also seen situations where a moving-ball penalty was not justified even though a player thought he'd incurred one and called it on himself. That is the price a golfer risks if he won't learn the rules.

How to Compete at Stroke Play

2. The rules prohibit you from asking an opponent any question that might assist you in playing a shot—like what club he used. But the rules *don't* stop you from noticing the clubs your opponents use, or watching how their shots behave. I try never to intrude myself on opponents, but at the same time I watch them pretty carefully any time I think I might learn something. The most obvious place is on the putting green. Simply being observant can aid you on many other shots, particularly with wind and ground conditions.

1. Most great players consider the golf course to be their opposition much more than their fellow competitors. This is particularly true of stroke play, where the result may not be decided until the last putt on the final green. Only in special circumstances should you let the standing of other players figure in your stroke-play game plan. Yet you never should hesitate to *observe* their efforts, because you can learn things that will help you.

3. It's difficult not to look back and ahead, but the less you do in stroke play, the better you'll play in the long run. Stroke play is an *18-hole game,* but you can play it only *one shot at a time.* Invariably you'll have some success and some failure, but the less you react emotionally to both, the less your risk of either playing too cautiously or gambling too hard. I fight a continual battle with myself to play neither too protectively following a hot stretch nor too boldly following a poor one. I do this by trying to concentrate only on the shot at hand, without relating that shot to what has passed or to what lies ahead.

When you're in cohtention toward the end of a stroke-play event you must be highly ware of your opponents to judge what has to be attempted ith any particular hot. For example, in his year's Masters I'd etermined at the final ole simply to try to et my second shot nto the green within afe two-putt range, nd I was actually tepping up to the shot when I heard the roar or Tom Watson's birde on 17. There was no way not to respond diectly to that. I had to o for the flag and a irdie. The replanned hot was a riskier one nd I didn't bring it off, eaving the ball in a unker, but the misake was in the physial execution, not the trategy.

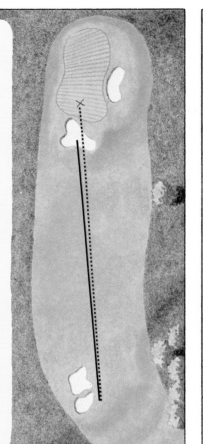

5. You really have to bear down on not playing the other guy in stroke play when there is some sort of personal relationship between you, or he's the fellow most likely to beat you and he's right there alongside you. It always has been very tough for Arnold Palmer and me to play our own games when we're paired together. Too often we've both lost out by letting ourselves get caught up in the "shoot-out" mentality of the fans. I'm sure this happens a lot between friends or archrivals in club golf. An even more common example is trying for more distance than you're capable of to stay up with a long hitter. A realistic attitude and self-discipline are the only answers to these problems.

6. I've never been too proud to admit that a number of my major championships were more the result of others losing than me winning with spectacular golf down the stretch. My one-shot-at-a-time, keep-cool, golf's-an-18-hole-game attitude has had a lot to do with whatever success I've had—and never more so than in one year's Tournament of Champions. I was tired and still "down" after a close Masters loss, the course was difficult to score on, I had my upcoming Memorial Tournament very much on my mind, and my driver felt like a warped pool cue—I hit only 15 fairways with it in the four rounds. But with nine holes to play I found I was still in contention despite all the scraping and scratching I'd had to do. That, of course, produces a lot of resolution and adrenalin, and I got into a playoff with Bruce Lietzke. Then, suddenly, I was able to find the fairway with a drive or two and, bingo, I'd achieved a most unexpected win. There was no way that would have happened if I'd let myself dwell on the shots I had already hit or the ones I was going to have to hit later. I consciously made myself play one shot at a time.

Lesson 8:

How to Win at Match Play

1. A golfer's greatest single asset is confidence in his own game, and it is particularly critical in match play. Most of the time in stroke play, you don't actually see what your opponents are doing, and you can keep your mind on your own game. In match play you are confronted throughout, close up, with the player you have to beat, and if you don't win you know it's goodbye. In those circumstances, the level of confidence you can sustain in your own capabilities is frequently the decisive factor.

2. Because confidence is such a factor in match play, good scramblers do well at it. Walter Hagen, who won a record five PGA Championships playing man-to-man golf, once said that he *expected* to make at least seven bad shots a round. What he didn't add is that he also had total confidence about recovering from most of them with some sort of cleverly manufactured shot or a long putt. I never played Walter, but I've run into a few golfers who, like him, had total faith in their ability to continually get the ball up and down from strange places—who, in fact, *based* their games on that ability much more than on, say, long, straight driving. These are the toughest of all match play opponents because of their demoralizing effect on you. There you go striking the ball sweetly and placing it accurately, and there they go, matching or bettering your scores with what looks like a mad combination of fluke shots and lucky bounces. The easiest mistake to make in such circumstances is to believe that those shots really are lucky and that they must come to an end. Lacking experience, I definitely made that mistake against Harvie Ward in the second round of the 1958 U.S. Amateur at Olympic in San Francisco. Harvie hit only five greens that day, but every time he stood over his ball with the putter, in it went. I couldn't believe this could continue—until suddenly we'd played the 18th and I was still 1 down. Since then I've learned that a much better approach is to accept what a fine scrambler the fellow is, *expect* him to keep on being one, and do your darnedest to beat him by sticking to your own game plan. If you fail, make the loss work for you by spending more practice time on your own recovery-shot repertoire.

3. One mistake I suspect weekenders frequently make in match play is trying to strike the ball and score beyond their capabilities when confronting better golfers. Wanting to raise your game to an opponent's level is a natural instinct—and worth pursuing on the practice tee—but it will produce nothing but heartache in competition if he's a 4-handicapper and you're an 18. Don't play to impress him —play to *win*. Use whatever handicap strokes you get to maximum effect through smart course management and shot strategy. Unless you are forced to gamble by the threat of being closed out, always assess and play the percentages: for instance, go only for *net* pars on holes where your opponent can have problems making gross pars.

4. A definite time to be conservative in match play is when your opponent, hitting first, finds serious trouble such as out-of-bounds. Swallow your pride and play it cozy, not just to win the hole but to protect against the psychological trauma that results from not capitalizing on a "gift" situation. Conversely, if you're in trouble and he's obviously in A-1 shape, there's little to be lost by gambling. The percentages are that you'll lose the hole anyway, and if the gamble comes off and you halve or win the hole, it's he who suffers the emotional jolt.

5. In match play don't ever let yourself become demoralized or forced out of your accustomed swing pattern by a long hitter. Long hitting in match play can be a double-edged sword. Certainly if the other guy is 20 yards ahead of you off the tee he's going to be able to use a shorter club to the green. But if you're on the green first—and especially if you're in one-putt range—then his shot becomes harder, no matter how good a player he is or what club he's using. That's why being outhit has never much bothered me in match play.

6. Before any serious match play encounter, make a point of holing out all those little putts that are so often "gimmes" in friendly Saturday-morning games. Nearly 20 years ago in the 36-hole final of the North and South Amateur at Pinehurst, a fine California golfer, Gene Andrews, and I were fighting tooth and nail for a lead coming to the end of the morning 18. On the 15th hole I half expected Gene to concede my two-foot putt, but, instead, he walked to the next tee. I missed it. I scraped through in that final, but since then I have never expected a putt to be conceded.

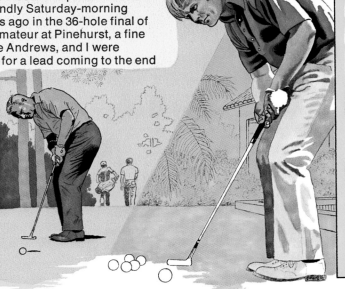

7. Throughout my career I've tried hard to avoid any act that could be construed as "gamesmanship." Maybe it's possible to do or say borderline things that could give you an edge over the other guy and still be able to live with yourself, but for me it's not. I want to win very badly, but I want to win only with my clubs. I neither practice gamesmanship personally nor have much respect for players who do. One benefit is that other golfers rarely if ever try gamesmanship on me. I think if you follow the same policy you'll derive the same benefit. And you won't be distracted from your basic objective of playing your best.

Combating Pressure

1. However it may look from outside the ropes, I feel pressure, just as you do. One of the worst bouts of nervousness I can recall came the final day of the 1967 U.S. Open at Baltusrol. I made a dumb bogey on 10 and suddenly was full of self-doubt, even though I was still leading by three shots. I'd found many times before when fear started to hit me that my best chance of overcoming it lay in facing it squarely and examining it rationally. Often I do that by actually talking to myself. Here's what I said inside my head at Baltusrol: "OK, what are you frightened of? You've obviously played well or you wouldn't be here. You're still playing well overall. You're always telling yourself you get your biggest kicks out of the challenges of golf. Well, go ahead and enjoy yourself. Play each shot one at a time and meet the challenge." It worked then and it has calmed me down many times since. I believe a similar sort of internal pep talk might also help you whenever you get into one of those throat-tightening situations.

2. Concentration is another fine antidote to anxiety. I have always felt that the sheer *intensity* Ben Hogan applied to the shotmaking specifi was one of his greatest assets. It left no room in his mind for negative thoughts. The busier you can keep yourself with the particulars of sho assessment and execution, the less chance your mind has to dwell on the emotional "if" and "but" factors that breed anxiety. We don't all have Ben's enormous self-discipline, but we all can go through a set of positive thought beginning with observing and evaluating the shot and ending with some sort of internal rehearsal of the technique we intend to apply. The more you make a habit of going through these shotmaking specifics, in non-pressure situations the less room there wil be in your mind for fear-producing thoughts under pressure.

3. The more "charged up" yo are, the harder you will hit the ball. Learn to allow for that. Fo example, in the 1967 U.S. Ope already mentioned I came to t 582-yard final hole with a four-shot lead and very conscious that a birdie would give me the Open 72-hole record. Water ahead plus my adrenalin flow led me to lay up off the tee, and after a second iron shot I was still 235 yards from the pin. Normally this would have been a light 3-wood, but in my highly "pumped" condition I knew I'd give the shot extra juice. So I h a 1-iron which, when it made th heart of the green, got me so elated that I became extremely positive about the putt, and I sank it. Understanding the affects of adrenalin flow paid o

4. Play the percentages under pressure. Don't allow your ego to tempt you into trying to do more than you actually have to. For example, if you're leading by three strokes coming down the last hole and the pin is tucked tight behind a water hazard, the percentages favor playing away from it, even though you might leave yourself a chip or long putt. Then on either of those shots, the odds favor lagging, not bravado. In other words, ease the pressure on yourself by playing the *least risky* shot possible. You'll probably find it easier to do if you keep in mind that, 10 minutes after you've won, no one will remember *how* you won. But if you lose when you should have won, a lot of people will know why.

5. Pressure creates tension, and when you're tense you want to get your task over and done with as fast as possible. The more you hurry in golf, the worse you probably will play, which leads to even heavier pressure and greater tension. I try to avoid this vicious circle in two ways. First, I'll take a couple of deep breaths and quickly review why I'm doing what I'm doing. Basically, I'm doing it because, win or lose, I enjoy *playing* golf and competing. This usually eases any mental tension I'm feeling by re-establishing my perspectives on victory and defeat in relation to life in the whole. Then to ease the tension and get my mind back on the game, I'll make two or three full practice swings concentrating on tempo rather than mechanics. The more smoothly and deliberately I can make each swing, the lower my tension level becomes.

6. Every good golfer possesses a carefully developed set of key swing thoughts that he uses to keep his game in balance. Generally one thought will be especially helpful in combating pressure. The one that has been the most beneficial over the years to me is, interestingly enough, also the simplest. The thought is: "Complete the backswing." Like most other golfers, I have a tendency to start coming down before I've finished going up any time tension begins to shorten and stiffen my muscles. By thinking "Complete the backswing," I remind myself to wait for the feeling that I've completed my turn and maximized my arm extension. The thought also has a good effect on my overall tempo, because I know I can't achieve that feeling if I don't swing smoothly and deliberately.

Principles of Position Play

1. As a breed, weekend golfers are too preoccupied with power and far too little concerned with position. Example? The card says par 4, so, with hardly a glance down the fairway, Joe climbs up on the tee with a driver in his hand and for the one time this month produces his Sunday punch. "Wow!" he says to the rest of the group as the ball rifles away. "I really nailed that one!" When he gets to the ball, it's 20 yards ahead of everybody else. But he also carried the brow of a hill and he now faces a long-iron shot from a severe downhill lie. He'd have been better off 20 yards shorter. There's at least one Joe in every foursome, and you can always recognize him. He's the guy reaching for his wallet.

2. If I approached golf as thoughtlessly and impulsively as the Joes of the world, I'd still be selling insurance for a living. Long ago, fortunately, I learned a lesson that seems to escape many people who play the game for fun—and even a few who play for a living: There is an *ideal route* for playing every golf hole ever built, and the more precisely you can identify it, the greater your chances of success. Obviously, that ideal route varies from player to player depending on his or her ability, and it varies with weather and ground conditions. But it does exist—every day on every hole for every golfer. Training and disciplining yourself to identify *your* ideal route before hitting would help your score more than any other single golfing attribute you could acquire.

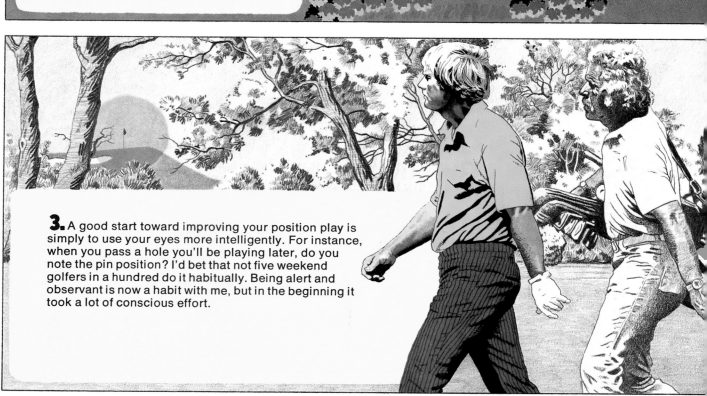

3. A good start toward improving your position play is simply to use your eyes more intelligently. For instance, when you pass a hole you'll be playing later, do you note the pin position? I'd bet that not five weekend golfers in a hundred do it habitually. Being alert and observant is now a habit with me, but in the beginning it took a lot of conscious effort.

4. Before every tee shot, *look hard* at what confronts you and then decide on a club and a target. Evaluate the specific risks, weighing the severity of each hazard against your capabilities. Here is my own risk rating of hazards in diminishing order: out-of-bounds, water, unplayable lie, steep-lipped bunker, heavy rough, severe ground slope, shallow-lipped bunker, light rough, slight ground slope. Determine your risk ratings according to your own strengths and weaknesses.

5. If you observe and evaluate thoroughly, your mind will automatically compute a target picture. Don't accept it if you would have to hit the best shot of your life to reach the target. Run all the information through again, asking your mind for more realism and for a reasonable *area* of fairway rather than a specific spot. The greater realism is necessary because the odds are extremely high against hitting the best shot of your life. The area is necessary because no one is good enough at golf to hit a specific spot. By trying to do so you put your swing under needless extra pressure.

NO

YES

J McQueen

6. Once you've computed a realistic target area, "Go to the movies." Picture first the flight of the ball as it will move from the clubhead to the target —track the ball's flight just as you will after you actually hit it. Pick the ball up in your mind's eye about 50 yards out and watch it soar and fall right into the heart of the target area you're actually looking at. As soon as it has "landed," change mental images again. This time, sense the feel of the swing that will send the ball flying just as you've visualized. Do that a couple of times, at least. Undoubtedly a club selection will suggest itself, if it didn't already. Take the club from the bag, put your best grip on it, aim and align yourself, and play away.

Lesson 11:
Slopes and Elevations

1. The more level the lie, the easier the game. Keep that in mind in evaluating every shot, beginning on the tee. Don't just mindlessly stick the ball midway between the markers, as so many players do. Seek out the most level patch of ground you can find in the teeing area that complements your intended shot. Remember that you can tee the ball up to two club-lengths behind the markers, and that only the ball (not yourself) has to be within the markers. If a poorly-built tee makes a slope unavoidable, then adjust your aim and setup accordingly. If the ground slopes away from you, it will promote a fade or slice. If it slopes toward you, there will be a tendency to draw or hook.

2. Take into account slopes, as well as hazards and approach angles, in *all* your shot planning. The less level the lie, the worse your percentages become, irrespective of distance. For instance, I'd much rather play a 5-iron from a level stance than an 8-iron from a severe slope—which is why you'll often see me hitting an iron rather than a wood from the tee on undulating courses. I want a level lie for the next shot. Especially avoid *downhill* lies. If you think you might clear the crest of a hill with a driver and leave yourself a downhill lie, then go for the crest with a 3- or 4-wood. That way, even if you come up short, you'll still have an easier approach from the uphill lie than you would from the downhill slope.

3. Consider sideslopes as carefully as upslopes and downslopes. If a hole curves left and the fairway slopes from right to left, leveling out as it goes, the intelligent place to aim is to the *right* side of the fairway. That way you use the slope positively in three ways: (1) to increase distance by obtaining maximum roll from the slope's banking effect, (2) to bounce the ball in the direction of the fairway curve, and (3) to run the ball toward the level left half of the fairway. Reverse strategy applies for the reverse situation.

4. Learn also to study the ground's *elevation.* Let's use an actual example from the pro tour to make a point about the *height* of your target. The 16th hole at Whitemarsh Valley C.C. in Philadelphia is 145 yards long—normally 7-iron distance for most pros. But a survey one year showed that a majority of the players went with a 6-iron. Why? Because, as the dotted line shows, *the higher the target, the shorter the arc of the shot and the sooner the ball lands.* A 7-iron shot would easily travel the required distance on level terrain, but it would land well short on this hole.

5. The eighth hole at Muirfield Village—my favorite among the par 3s there—exemplifies the opposite effect. Here the green is well below the level of the tee, which means that with any given club *the arc of the shot will be extended and the ball will travel farther than it would over level land.* The strategy for both situations becomes clear: The higher the target, the *more* club you need; the lower the target, the *less* club it takes to reach it, other considerations being equal. How much more or less? My rule of thumb is one club for each 30 feet of elevation or depression.

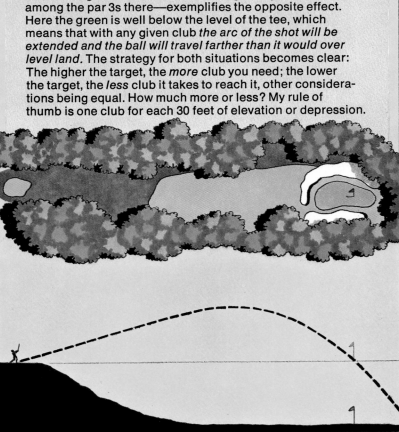

J. McQueen

"Manufacturing" Shots by Using Your Imagination

1. Your powers of observation are your first strategic weapon. Second is your imagination. There is an ideal way to play almost every shot in golf. The better you can identify and imagine it, the greater your scoring chances become. Obviously, you won't always execute a shot the way you've pictured it, but don't let that divert you from going through the mental exercise. Make a habit of fitting shots to situations in your mind's eye, because you at least give yourself a positive goal. If the ideal shot exceeds your physical capabilities, then figure out the nearest approximation that you have a reasonable chance of executing.

2. One reason I enjoy British links golf so much is the need to "manufacture" shots, as the locals describe it. You are not a complete golfer to Scottish fans— the most discerning in the world—until you can tailor your play to whatever circumstance you find yourself in. For example, the pitch-and-run is an essential shot on every linksland course, and I've rescued many a score with it on the U.S. tour. I expect the shot will come in handy in the upcoming British Open at St. Andrews. Play the shot with a less-lofted club, and figure on rolling the ball about as far as you fly it. Use this shot anywhere from 80 yards in when the ground is firm and fairly level and there are no hazards between you and the pin.

3. Here's a classic situation where a little forethought and imagination can save you a lot of pain. This is the sixth hole at Muirfield Village, requiring a long approach for most players. Generally their dominant thought will be getting over the water, so they hit a hard-driving shot with a long iron. But the green here is relatively shallow and firm, and frequently a well-struck shot will skate through the green and into the rough behind it. Most amateurs can manage a fade, and that's the shot an alert pair of eyes and an active imagination ought to suggest. Played with, say, a 5-wood instead of a 2- or 3-iron, the extra height and backspin imparted to the ball will give it stopping power.

4. Tailoring shots to situations requires a knowledge of golf's basic cause-and-effect factors. Height and curve are the primary considerations. For a low, hard-running shot, move the ball back at address, close the clubface slightly and keep your hands ahead of the clubhead. Allow for a draw or hook. For a high shot, set the ball forward in your stance, open the clubface a bit, and throw the clubhead well under the ball by fully releasing your hands and wrists through impact. Allow for a fade or slice. For a deliberate draw or hook, aim your shoulders and feet right of target, close the clubface and swing normally. Allow for a lower-flying shot and more distance than usual.

5. A fertile imagination pays off most in the short game, because here the scope for manufacturing shots is almost infinite. I've been playing golf for more than 25 years, but I still never go a month without learning some new wrinkle about chipping, pitching or sand play—which is one reason I built a practice green and bunker in my backyard. Gary Player, one of golf's greatest shot manufacturers, once told me he didn't think there was any situation in golf where the ball couldn't be got within one-putt range so long as it could be struck fairly cleanly. The key to getting it there is in the imagination. Then you need the delicacy of "touch" and degree of confidence bred by experimenting and practice. Get yourself a bag of balls and a handful of clubs and see if you can't build this ability into your game.

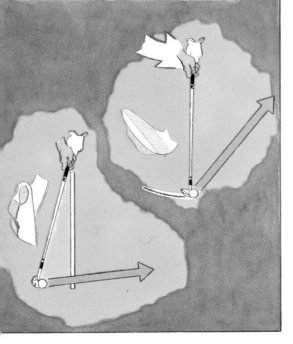

How to Target Your Shots

1. Driving-range practice can do the average golfer more harm than good. Certainly working on good swing mechanics is helpful, but because a range is so expansive and penalty-free, beating balls can lead to sloppy aiming habits. The shrunken confines of a golf course, much more than sudden collapses of swing form, cause many players to lose their driving-range games almost as soon as they face the real thing. The answer lies in becoming more *target-conscious*. Make it a rule from today on *never* to hit a shot without a specific, clearly-identified target in mind, both on the course and in practice. That's been a rule of mine since I was 15, and it's one I have *never* broken.

2. The first target to identify on the course is off the tee. Start by selecting the fairway *area* in which you want the ball to finish, considering the lie of the land, ground conditions, pin position, hazards that could come into play, wind conditions—*and your own capabilities.* Virtually every hole in golf offers any level of golfer a preferred driving area. Make identifying yours your first task on every tee, *before* you take a club or tee your ball. Next, give yourself a line through the center of your driving area by identifying a marker beyond it—a tree or a tower or the edge of a distant trap. Now take the club you feel will hit the ball to the center of the area you've defined, aim and align on your marker, and swing *freely.* You may not do what you've planned every time, but you'll find the *positiveness* of your routine will help dispel doubt and fear.

3. OK, let's suppose you did what you planned on the tee and are in Position A on the fairway and have a 5-iron to an 80-foot-wide green with the pin set in the center. Let's also suppose that your natural shot shape—the curve you hit 90 percent of the time—is a fade/slice, from left to right. Consider the following before you hit. If you aim directly at the pin, you have 40 feet of green on either side to work with should you "miss" the shot. You will be left with a hefty putt at best. Now see what happens instead if you *allow* for your fade/slice by aiming, say, 20 feet left of the pin. If you hit the shot you've planned and the distance is exact, you are in the hole. If, miraculously, you drill the ball dead straight, you are only 20 feet left of the hole. If you double the amount of fade you'd planned, you are only 20 feet to the right of the hole. By playing the percentages of your own tendencies, you double your margin for error.

4. How much curve should you allow for in fading or drawing the ball to the target? Your own experience will answer that question better than I can, but here as a guide are my own criteria for left-to-right shots when I'm playing at my peak. From the tee, I allow for the ball to swing about half the width of the fairway, and I aim for the left edge so I'm still on short grass if I happen to drive the ball straight. With a 3-iron I'll usually aim 20 to 30 feet left of the pin; with a 5-iron 15 to 20 feet left; with an 8-iron about 10 feet left; with a wedge just a shade left. In establishing your own allowances, remember that the more lofted the club, the more difficult it is to fade or draw the ball. Remember also that a ball you draw from right to left flies lower and lands harder and faster than a fade.

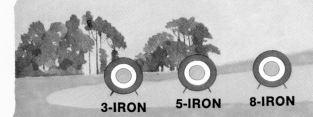

3-IRON   **5-IRON**   **8-IRON**

5. I dislike blind shots intensely, but I don't let them disrupt my game plan. There are two problems any time you can't see where you are going: how far to hit and where to hit. The only way to solve them is to have a quick look. Generally I already know the yardage I have to cover because I will have paced it out and noted it in practice. If for some reason I haven't been able to do that, I determine it by first estimating the distance from the target to the point where it comes fully into view, then adding the distance from that point back to the ball. To establish the line, I select a tree or other tall object directly behind my target area, and keep careful track of it walking back to the ball. If no skyline marker is available, I identify an aiming point on the crest of the hill.

Lesson 14:
Driving Strategy

1. Treating the tee shot as a routine chore to be done with little forethought is a common—and costly—mistake among high handicappers. You don't just step up and casually slap a putt in the general direction of the hole. You analyze, plan and concentrate on a specific target. Do the same on your drives. Your basic objective on all par-4 and par-5 tee shots is to land the ball in the part of the fairway that establishes the easiest possible second shot, taking into account your shotmaking capabilities. Assess the hole in those terms while others are playing, or by proceeding promptly to the tee if you are up first. Having clearly determined what you are going to attempt, mentally picture the swing you will make and the flight of the ball as you select the club that will achieve your goal. As you finally assemble your setup, switch your mind to *one* key swing thought and go.

2. There are four primary considerations in determining the easiest possible second shot. The first is hazards. In assessing how closely you should flirt with a hazard from the tee, always ask yourself whether the possible reward is worth the risk involved. Very often the intelligent golfer will decide that it isn't, especially when he is under pressure or doesn't need to take undue chances. The second consideration is the angle of approach to the pin, or to the ideal area from which to play the third shot if the green can't be reached in two. On most well-designed courses, one half of the fairway offers a clearer, easier shot to the pin. The third consideration is the lie of the ball. The more sloping it is, in any direction, the more difficult your shot becomes, which is why I will almost always sacrifice distance from the tee to get a level lie (and I make sure my stance on the tee is level, too). The fourth consideration is wind. Basically with wind you have two choices: either to work the ball against it by imparting a particular spin, or to allow for its effect when you aim.

3. Understand that distance off the tee is of value only in relation to position; there are no prizes for long driving in and of itself. A ball hit straight down the middle often will finish closer to the green than a ball traveling farther but finishing off to the side. Consider also that a ball landing on short fairway grass often will roll for good extra distance, whereas a ball landing in long grass won't. In other words, don't be a slugger just for the ego trip. Back in 1966 I won my first British Open at the 6,892-yard Muirfield course in Scotland hitting my driver only 17 times on 56 par-4 and par-5 holes, because of the heavy rough and dry fairways. Others hit the ball way past me, but that didn't cause me to change what I believed was the proper game plan under those circumstances. Nor should a longer hitter in your Saturday morning foursome change your plan.

4. There are times, though, when every golfer should go for maximum distance off the tee, and learning to recognize them is basic to becoming a good strategist. A perfect example in the case of the tour pros is the 15th at Augusta National. Almost everyone cuts loose here because the reward can be a shot at the green with an iron for a two-putt birdie, and the penalty if the drive wanders is generally no more than a lay-up short of the water for a pitch on and possible one-putt birdie or two-putt par. You should go for the big drive on long par-4 and par-5 holes that are open and trouble-free. Catch one really solid and you give yourself the chance of a birdie or an easy par. Miss the drive a little and you still can put your second shot up in front of the green.

5. Here are a couple of tips to help you hit that extra big drive. The speed of my leg and hip action on the forward swing is a big factor in how much club-head speed I generate and how far I hit the ball. When I'm letting it all out, I make a slight stance adjustment that helps me increase my speed. I angle my left foot a little more toward the hole than normal. The effect is to give myself a sort of "running start" in shifting my legs toward the target and unwinding my hips on the downswing. If that doesn't work for you, try this. Relax your entire body before you address the ball, then step up and swing with a minimum of delay after you've completed your setup.

J McQueen

The Not-So-Simple Art of Teeing Up

1. A basic of good golf strategy is seizing every advantage the game offers you. You can grasp several in the seemingly simple act of teeing the ball, although most players unwittingly ignore them. As a general principle, tee the ball so that you aim and hit *away* from the worst potential trouble area. For example, if a hole has bunkers down the left side of the fairway but out-of-bounds tight down the right side, then peg the ball on the *right* side of the tee and hit for the *left* half of the fairway. If you catch the sand it *may* cost you a shot, but if you go out-of-bounds it *definitely* will cost you two shots (stroke and distance). Conversely, when the more severe trouble, water perhaps, lies to the left, tee up left and aim and hit away from it. Other things being equal, you generally will get more distance in crosswinds by letting the air currents keep the ball flying longer. Tee up left and aim down the left side of the fairway when the wind is from left to right, and do the reverse when the wind is from right to left. As I've said before, and it bears repeating, it's important to find a level area on the tee from which to play. In seeking out such an area, remember that the ball may be teed anywhere between the markers and to a depth of two club-lengths behind them.

2. In 1955 Ben Hogan came to the last tee of an 18-hole playoff for the U.S. Open at the Olympic Club in San Francisco, one shot behind Jack Fleck. A win would have given Ben a record fifth U.S. Open title, and he needed a birdie to have a chance of tieing Fleck and going another 18 holes. The 18th at Olympic is a comparatively short par 4, normally an easy hole for the greatest golfer of his day. But the surface of the tee was dry and loamy, and on his drive Ben's right foot slipped, causing him to hit the ball into deep rough from where it took him three shots to get back onto the fairway. He later described the experience as one of his greatest disappointments in golf, but he blamed no one but himself. "I should have worked my feet into the soil," he said, "just like you do in a sand trap. But I didn't."

J. McQueen

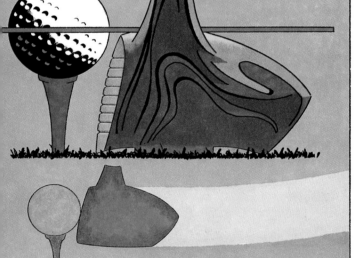

3. My policy on almost all normal driver shots is to tee the ball at the same height—the height where I can catch it exactly at the bottom of the swing arc or very slightly on the upswing. One theory—erroneous, in my opinion—is that the ball should be teed higher for a high shot and lower for a low shot. I don't buy that as a general rule, for two reasons. First, unless you possess the skills of a Ben Hogan, varying the height of the ball for a driver shot forces you to change your swing path and that breeds inconsistency. Second, teeing the ball lower than normal promotes a steeper angle of clubhead approach that imparts more backspin to the ball and diminishes the forward thrust of the club, causing the ball to soar higher and fall shorter. In my case, the ball is at its proper height when its center is about opposite the top edge of the driver face when the club is grounded.

4. I often see golfers teeing up on short holes where they are using less than a driver simply toss the ball down and hit it from the grass. You'll never see me do that, for the simple reason that I don't believe in giving myself the possibility of a mediocre lie when I'm allowed a perfect one. On *every* tee, whatever the club or the shot, I set the ball on a peg. Usually, the longer the club and the higher I want to fly the ball, the higher I tee the ball. That way I eliminate the possibility of grass reducing backspin and also reduce the chance of hitting behind the ball.

How to Deal with Different Grasses

1. Different grass types and conditions require different shotmaking approaches. Don't let a high handicap or doubt about your ability to finesse the ball persuade you to ignore or discount these important "lie" considerations. Rule No. 1 in tackling varying turf conditions concerns the length and texture of the grass immediately behind the ball. The longer and/or lusher it is, the more it will be trapped between the clubface and the ball at impact, which lessens the backspin you impart. Reduced backspin produces two effects. One is the ball's lower and greater forward momentum, resulting in increased distance — the "flier" as it is known and hated on the pro tour. The other is a shallower landing trajectory and less "bite." Generally, you'll want to try for a higher shot with a more lofted club. Sidespin also is reduced by grass between ball and clubface, which makes it harder to hook or slice. This is especially true when you are playing out of rough. When in a particularly heavy lie, don't be fancy—play for a more or less straight shot.

BERMUDA   **BENT**

YES

NO

McQueen

2. Go easy on the "winter rules." Improve your lie only when conditions force you to, unless you don't mind a drop in confidence when you suddenly have to observe the game's true rules in a match or a formal tournament. When you *must* move the ball, don't reveal a lack of golfing sophistication by sticking it on a big, fluffy tuft of grass. The ideal flight for all approach shots is a thrusting, slow-climbing shot that peaks sharply, then falls quietly to earth on an almost vertical trajectory. Such flighting is possible only from a firm, clean lie—which is why the pros enjoy well-maintained, tightly-mowed Bermuda grass and the fescue grasses of the British links. Try to find such a lie whenever you must move the ball.

3. Knowledge of grass species is a useful tactical weapon, especially on courses you're playing for the first time. For example, common Bermuda grass needs less water and usually grows on sand-based, well-drained ground. This means harder turf and lots of bounce and roll. Bent grass, Poa annua and bluegrass, basics in the Northern regions, need heavy watering in hot weather. So they frequently have a soft base, which limits roll even when they are cut short. When the blades of these Northern grasses are long or wet, you get "fliers" and less backspin. Again, you need a more lofted club and, ideally, a fade instead of a draw on shots to the green. If you don't recognize what you are playing on, a word with the pro or course superintendent before going out might save you a shot or two by identifying the conditions you can expect.

4. The short game is where knowledge of grass and shotmaking finesse pay off best. As a rule of thumb, the coarser the blades and the more thickly matted the grass (Bermuda, for example), the greater the tendency to stick the club in the ground on short pitch or chip shots. Concentrate on *accelerating* the club through, not just to, the ball with a firm, positive swing. You can sometimes get away with a quitting action on soft grasses by bouncing the clubhead through the ball, but you rarely will on the tougher Southern turfs. Also, play for the ball to stop quicker and run less on coarser-bladed, more finely matted greens—particularly into upslopes. Save those pitch-and-runs for the fine-bladed bents and fescues. Carry the ball well up toward the hole on short shots from Bermuda.

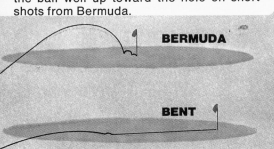

BERMUDA

BENT

5. Learn to take the grain of the green into account on short shots on Bermuda—particularly in putting. Remember that all Bermuda grasses grow toward the setting sun, and that most softer grasses like bent and Poa annua follow the direction of the drainage. Look around as you approach each green to determine east and west or where the land lies lowest. If you suspect the grain isn't behaving as it should, check the appearance of the grass—the grain runs away from you when the surface looks shiny and toward you when it looks dull. Bermuda generally has a more pronounced grain than the Northern grasses, but don't take any chances — Northern grass can become grainy enough to move a seemingly straight three-foot putt well wide of the hole, especially when the grass becomes a little shaggy late on a good growing day.

Lesson 17:
Driving on Doglegs

1. Dogleg holes need special planning, particularly when they bend acutely. Direction obviously is a critical factor, but so is distance. What is more frustrating than striking the ball solidly, then watching it fly or roll through the corner of the dogleg into trouble? I've even seen tour pros make that mistake, but the ones who do it often aren't the names you see in the headlines. Doglegs demand astute club selection based on knowledge of distances—the course's and your own. So here's dogleg rule No. 1: If you think the driver *might* put you through the elbow of the dogleg, take a club you *know* will not no matter how well you hit it.

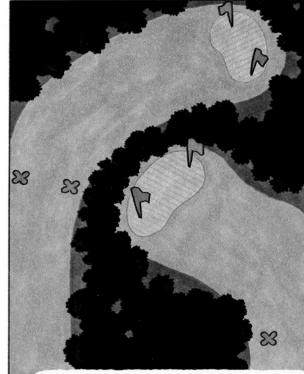

2. Knowing the pin position before you plan your tee shot is a fundamental of golfing strategy. It's never more important than on a dogleg, where the green probably is hidden from the tee. Tour caddies get us that information on preround course inspections. If you can't do that, at least make every effort to note upcoming pin locations as you play along. You are looking for the best angle of approach. If the hole doglegs to the right and the pin is on the right, then the *left* side of the fairway generally will offer the best angle. But if the pin on a left-to-right hole is on the left, your best angle likely will result from cutting the corner as closely as possible. If you find trouble on the right, you still should have a shot directly across the fairway to the pin. The converse strategies apply when the hole doglegs to the left.

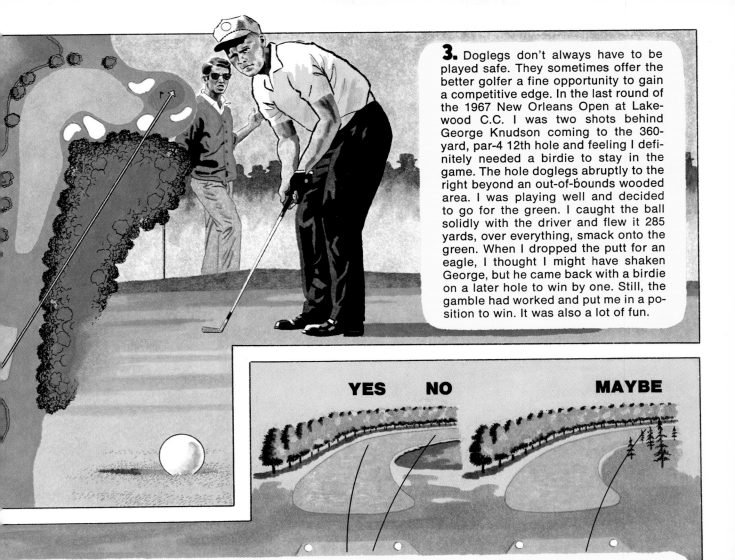

3. Doglegs don't always have to be played safe. They sometimes offer the better golfer a fine opportunity to gain a competitive edge. In the last round of the 1967 New Orleans Open at Lakewood C.C. I was two shots behind George Knudson coming to the 360-yard, par-4 12th hole and feeling I definitely needed a birdie to stay in the game. The hole doglegs abruptly to the right beyond an out-of-bounds wooded area. I was playing well and decided to go for the green. I caught the ball solidly with the driver and flew it 285 yards, over everything, smack onto the green. When I dropped the putt for an eagle, I thought I might have shaken George, but he came back with a birdie on a later hole to win by one. Still, the gamble had worked and put me in a position to win. It was also a lot of fun.

YES **NO** **MAYBE**

4. The keys to gambling on doglegs are recognizing your true capabilities and then minimizing the risks as much as possible. For example, if you don't normally fly the ball high with a driver, you shouldn't attempt to hit over tall trees with it. Use the 3-wood instead. If that's not enough club in terms of distance, then don't attempt the shot. Also, consider the consequences if you miss. If you face water or thick jungle or out-of-bounds, attempting to carry a corner may be sheer foolhardiness. On the other hand, if the worst you could encounter is light rough or a few well-spaced trees—*and you are playing well*—it can make sense to gamble.

5. If you have the ability to curve the ball either way at will, using that talent on doglegs will gain you some advantage. For instance, by aiming the ball down the left side and fading it toward the center of the fairway on holes that turn from left to right, you shorten your approach without risking corner cutting. You gain the same advantage by aiming down the right side and drawing the ball on holes that swing from right to left. But even if you have this "finessing" capability, keep in mind that distance is rarely all-important on an acute dogleg. These holes tend to be short, which means they generally have small, well-trapped greens. Your angle of approach is more critical than yardage.

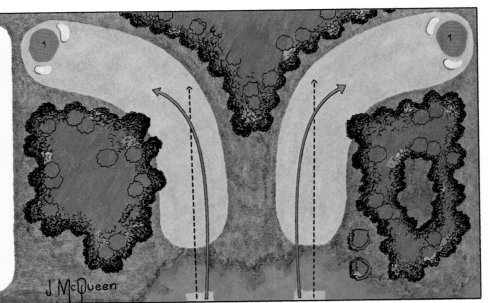

J McQueen

Distance Factors in Approaching

1. Don't be too ambitious with your approach shots. If you are a beginner or high handicapper, your goal on all approach shots should be to get the ball *anywhere* on the green, not next to the hole. If you're a middle-level player, a wise objective, until practice makes you a better striker of the ball, might be to get within reasonable two-putt distance as often as possible. Only if you are a skilled golfer —say 6-handicap or better— are you equipped to try to get within one-putt range, and then only when the percentages truly favor the attempt. Too conservative? No fun? Well, I'm a realist. In my book, it's either that or recognize and accept the penalties and frustrations that any other strategy is bound to exact.

18	in	total	handicap	net score
565	3671	7091		
525	3315	6561		
	36	72	32	
3	5	36	14	
			4	

2. Here's lesson No. 1 for anyone who wants to be a golfing realist. After each of your next three rounds, go over your card and figure out how many times you reached or passed the pin with your approach shots. If your handicap is 10 or more, I'll bet you were short of the hole at least two-thirds of the time. If your handicap is over 18, I wouldn't be surprised if you were short of the *green* at least a third of the time—even on your home course. Obviously, coming up short is costing you dearly. Why, then, do you keep repeating your error? In some cases the answer is pure ego: believing that you hit the ball farther than you do, or wanting to hit it farther than you can. Or else you assume that, because you hit a certain club perfectly a few times in the past, you are going to do it again every time you swing that club. The hard fact is that you are not. Golf at all levels is a game of misses. I rarely hit more than five or six shots exactly as I plan them even on my best days. On all approach shots I take a club that I believe will get me "up" even if I miss it slightly. In other words, I allow myself a margin for error. So should you on every shot into every green.

3. Try this if you're leaving your approach shots short. In your next five rounds, take *one more club* than you think you need for every approach shot and swing normally. You'll still misdirect a few shots, of course, but I think you'll learn a few things about golf that will greatly increase your enjoyment of the game. One is that the trouble behind greens is frequently less severe than the hazards in front of them, especially in regard to sand and water. A second is that you hit the ball straighter and more solidly when you don't mentally pressure yourself to produce absolute perfection and "press" every club for its maximum distance. Use one more club for at least five rounds, and I'm sure your handicap will drop.

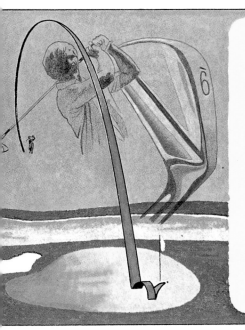

4. Next time you get a chance, make a point of studying the tour players on a short par 4, especially one with an elevated or hard green. Even though many of the pros conceivably could reach the putting surface with a driver, you generally will see them tee off with an iron or a fairway wood. One obvious reason is that short par 4s are frequently narrow and fraught with hazards. A less obvious reason is the difficulty of spinning the approach shot from a short distance. When they "lay up," the pros are giving themselves the chance to create more backspin by hitting a fuller approach shot, say a full 9-iron instead of a half wedge.

DOWNWIND

UPWIND

5. Golf downwind is definitely easier than when the air currents are dead in your face, but don't let the fun of hitting with the breeze fool you on approach shots. The stronger the wind in the direction of the shot, the "hotter" and lower it will fly and the harder and faster it will land. You need less club and more height. Move the ball a little forward at address and release fully through impact with your hands and wrists. The effect of a headwind, conversely, is to make the ball soar as its forward thrust weakens, calling for more club and a lower trajectory. Moving the ball back a little at address and keeping the hands well ahead of the clubface through impact will hold your shots down.

When to Gamble on Approach Shots

1. When should you gamble or not gamble? The specifics of each situation must be your final determinant, but it might help to keep in mind that there are many holes in any golfing contest, and it is a great shame to risk ruining your overall chances on any single one. Unless you are forced by the competitive situation to gamble, I lean toward playing safe and moving on. That's usually been my policy, and it's paid off—especially on the tough courses used in major championships. I suspect many higher handicappers don't play away from obvious danger because they've fallen into the habit of automatically aiming for the pin on all approach shots, irrespective of where it may be located or what may happen if the shot is missed somewhat. That kind of mental laziness is as much a cause of them remaining high handicappers as their lack of shotmaking skills. You *must* be analytical and you *must* be realistic to play this game well. For example, if big trouble lurks to one side of the green and that's where the pin is located, you should aim for the center and rely on your putting to do the rest. Tough as a 50-foot putt may be, it's usually a heck of a sight easier than a buried bunker shot or a tricky pitch from tall grass. And it *sure* beats a penalty stroke!

2. I was much less a thinking man's golfer as an amateur than I am these days, but even then I generally tried to use my mind ahead of my muscles. Playing the U.S. Open at Oakland Hills in 1961, I was very much in contention in the third round coming to the long par-4 18th, but missed my approach. The recovery choices were an extremely delicate shot over a deep, wide bunker and a mound, or a much safer shot skirting those hazards but hitting away from the pin. The temptation was enormous to go for the hole, but I chose the safe route, nearly sank the resulting 15-foot putt for a par, and went on to tie for fourth. Had I gambled and lost there I easily could have made 6 or 7, which would have had a very negative influence on my final day's play, apart from its immediate effect on my position.

3. Here's a technique basic to my game that I recommend to all golfers skilled enough to curve the ball either direction at will. It's called "working in from the middle." If the pin is to the far right side, aim to the center of the green and play a left-to-right fade. If the pin is to the extreme left, aim to the center of the green and play a right-to-left draw. By approaching this way, you frequently can get closer to the hole than you would by firing straight at the pin. Also, if your ball control is reasonably good, you increase your safety margin, because the shot is unlikely to bend so much you miss the green entirely. Should you "miss it straight," you're still in good shape in the middle of the green. Less skilled shotmakers can employ this tactic whenever the configuration of the hole matches their natural shot shape. For example, if you slice, aim to the left half of the green when the pin is to the right and let the ball drift toward the hole. If you hook, use the opposite tactic.

4. A moment ago I used the phrase "miss it straight," and may have puzzled golfers who thought the objective of the game was to hit the ball directly from A to B. Actually, it isn't —at least not at the highest levels of golf. Why not? Well, let's say I'm playing a 5-iron shot to a green 80 feet wide with the pin centrally located. If I aim at the pin and attempt to hit straight, I have only 40 feet of green to work with if I hook or slice the shot. But by aiming, say, 20 feet to the left or right of the pin and trying to fade or draw the ball in toward it, I give myself a much greater margin for error. Now I can "miss" the shot by 40 feet and still keep the ball within 20 feet of the hole. That is the tactical reason good golfers rarely try to hit the ball dead straight. The technical reason is that a straight shot is much harder to keep repeating than a fade or draw.

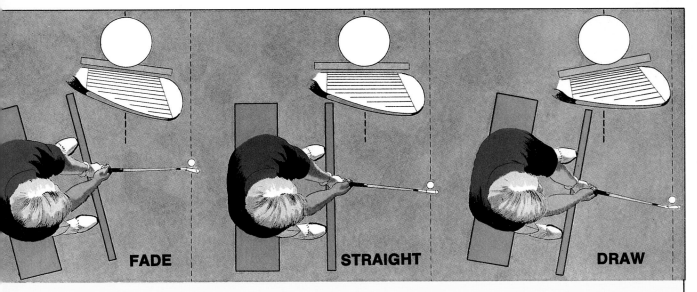

FADE   STRAIGHT   DRAW

5. No matter how good your swing, the ball won't go where you want it to unless you aim both the club and yourself correctly at the outset. The higher their handicaps, the less attention golfers seem to pay to this absolute fundamental. So, if you seem to be swinging well but find you are spraying your shots, check your clubface aim and your body alignment before you do anything else. If you want the ball to go dead straight (despite what I just said in the previous panel), your best chance will come with a clubface aimed squarely at the target and a body alignment—feet, knees, hips, shoulders —parallel to the target line. If you want the ball to fade, the clubface should look a little right of target at address and your body should align a little left of target. If you want to draw the ball, reverse those directions: face the club a little to the left of target and yourself to the right of it. Whatever shape of shot you want to play, success starts at address.

How to Get Out of Sand Every Time

1. Bunker play strategy starts with the right club and the right attitude. The right club is a sand wedge: a heavy-headed, highly-lofted iron with a flange that protrudes below the club's leading edge to prevent it from cutting too deeply into the sand. Bunker shots are possible with other clubs, but they *are almost always more difficult.* So if you don't have a sand wedge, get one. It represents one of your few chances to "buy" a better score. The right attitude is a positive and confident one, which requires knowledge and experience. Most golfers fear bunkers because they are unclear about the techniques for escaping them and never practice from sand. The basic technique for getting out of sand is to slide or knife or bounce the club through the sand beneath the ball. There are, however, many variations on that theme, and the more you know about them the better you'll play from bunkers. The best way to learn these techniques initially is via lessons, but sand shots are essentially "feel" shots, and there is no substitute for personal experiment and regular practice.

SW PW

2. Rule No. 1 of bunker strategy is: get out on your first attempt. Whenever I'm tempted to try anything too fancy from sand, I remind myself how leaving the ball in bunkers a couple of times at Merion in 1971 in a playoff with Lee Trevino cost me a U.S. Open. Some things are possible from bunkers and some things are not, and you should learn the difference and play accordingly. If you aren't sure, play safe. Be sure first of getting the ball back on short grass from a tough fairway bunker lie, even if doing that means you can't reach the green on your next shot. Similarly, make getting the ball somewhere on the putting surface your first priority from any kind of risky lie or awkward angle in a greenside bunker.

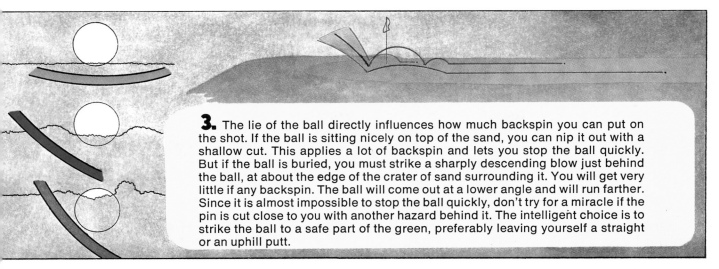

3. The lie of the ball directly influences how much backspin you can put on the shot. If the ball is sitting nicely on top of the sand, you can nip it out with a shallow cut. This applies a lot of backspin and lets you stop the ball quickly. But if the ball is buried, you must strike a sharply descending blow just behind the ball, at about the edge of the crater of sand surrounding it. You will get very little if any backspin. The ball will come out at a lower angle and will run farther. Since it is almost impossible to stop the ball quickly, don't try for a miracle if the pin is cut close to you with another hazard behind it. The intelligent choice is to strike the ball to a safe part of the green, preferably leaving yourself a straight or an uphill putt.

4. Your feet are great strategic weapons in bunkers. How you should attempt to play any given shot depends first on the texture and condition of the sand. The rules forbid you to test it with your hands or the club, but they say nothing about your feet. Use them along with your eyes as you walk into the bunker to sense the quality of the sand—its fineness or coarseness, its dryness or wetness. Wiggle your feet into the sand as you address the ball to confirm your initial impressions as well as to build a firm stance. As a general principle, the finer or drier the sand, the deeper the club will tend to bury in it and the more shallow you should attempt to cut beneath the ball or the more firmly you should swing.

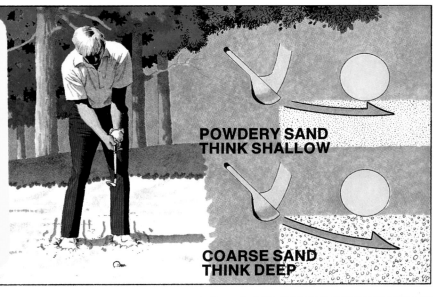

POWDERY SAND THINK SHALLOW

COARSE SAND THINK DEEP

5. The first thought of many high handicappers when they enter sand seems to be "Get it over with fast!" This is poor policy on any recovery shot, but it has two particularly bad effects in bunker play. One is a failure to do any green reading before hitting. Because short bunker shots are predominantly struck with an open clubface and an outside-in swinging action, they generally break from left to right on landing. Allowances need to be made for that in relation to green contours and speed. The second fault bred of anxiety is rushing the swing. Control of the club is paramount on every sand shot, and the slower and smoother your swing tempo the greater your club control is likely to be. In fact, this is so important to me I sometimes actually think of swinging in slow motion when playing out of sand.

Lesson 21:
Special Tactics for Sand Play

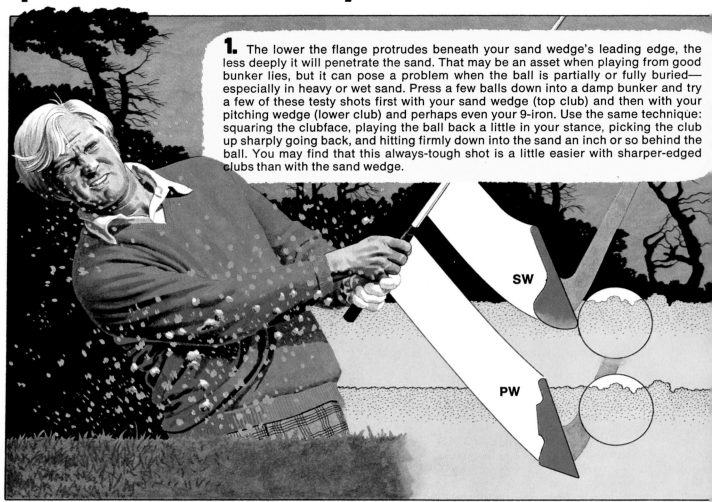

1. The lower the flange protrudes beneath your sand wedge's leading edge, the less deeply it will penetrate the sand. That may be an asset when playing from good bunker lies, but it can pose a problem when the ball is partially or fully buried—especially in heavy or wet sand. Press a few balls down into a damp bunker and try a few of these testy shots first with your sand wedge (top club) and then with your pitching wedge (lower club) and perhaps even your 9-iron. Use the same technique: squaring the clubface, playing the ball back a little in your stance, picking the club up sharply going back, and hitting firmly down into the sand an inch or so behind the ball. You may find that this always-tough shot is a little easier with sharper-edged clubs than with the sand wedge.

SW

PW

2. One factor that makes greenside bunker play difficult for less-skilled golfers is that these shots generally require less than a full-force swing. I sense that an uncertainty about how much oooomph to apply is a frequent cause of mishaps among my pro-am partners. What's the answer? Well, there really isn't a complete one beyond the innate "feel" that comes with experience and practice, but here's a mental yardstick that might help. On a normal explosion shot from a decent lie, think of hitting about twice as hard as you would on a pitch shot of the same distance. For instance, if the bunker shot has to travel 10 yards, swing as you would for a 20-yard pitch.

3. Chipping from sand requires confidence and a precise touch, but it can be a stroke-saver under certain conditions. I've generally attempted the shot only when the sand is firm, the lie is clean, the bunker has little or no lip, and the pin is so far away that judging the distance of an explosion shot would be quite difficult—which also means there'll be plenty of room for roll. To play the shot, set the ball back toward your right heel, choke down on your grip and then, with a *very* steady head, hit firmly down on the back of the ball, trying not to catch even a grain of sand until after impact. Practice this stroke before you try it in an important match or tournament.

4. Given the right conditions, putting out of sand also can be quite a percentage shot—and a less risky one than chipping for most players because there is less chance of catching the sand before the ball. The right conditions essentially are: little or no lip, a good lie, a flat bunker and firm or smooth sand. I find that addressing and striking the ball more toward the toe of the putter seems to increase its roll by reducing a tendency to skid. To make up for the off-center contact, grip and stroke a little more firmly than normal.

5. Practicing at Muirfield in Scotland before my first British Open win in 1966, I learned a most unusual sand tactic from Phil Rodgers. I didn't, as it turned out, have to use it in that particular championship, but it has come in handy on a number of occasions since. I'd never been able to figure out how to play a ball lying close to the back bank of a bunker when the bank was so steep I couldn't swing the club back normally. "What you do," said Rodgers, demonstrating, "is pick the club straight up in front of you, bending your arms as though you were chopping wood with an ax, then whack it down into the sand about two inches behind the ball as hard as you can with your right hand. The arc of the stroke is straight up and down, not back and forth as on all other shots. Don't worry about a follow-through because there won't be any—the clubhead has to bury in the sand." It's not the most elegant of strokes, but properly executed it will at least get the ball out most of the time, which in a situation like this is all that matters.

J McQueen

Long Bunker Shots

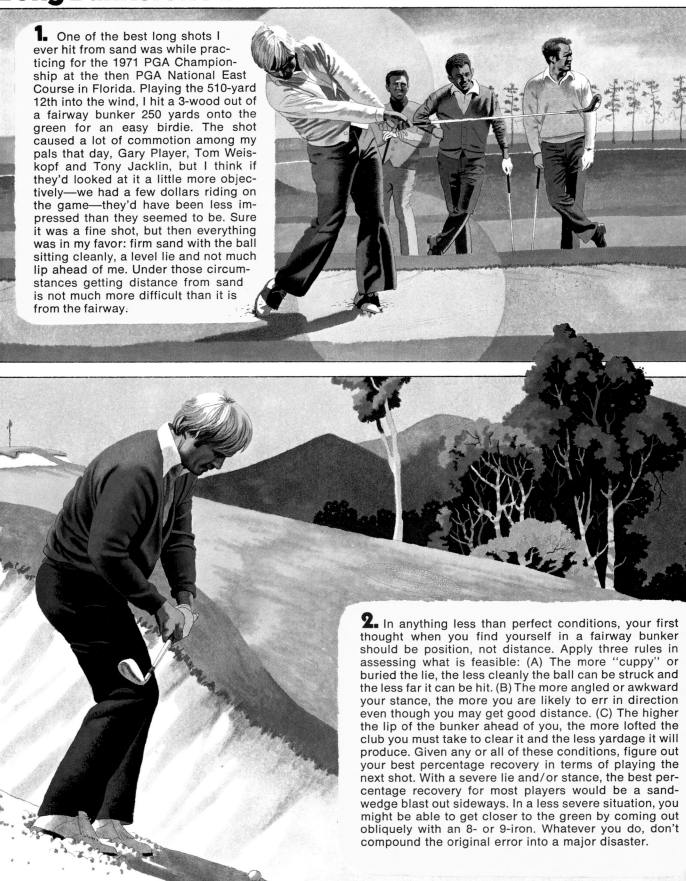

1. One of the best long shots I ever hit from sand was while practicing for the 1971 PGA Championship at the then PGA National East Course in Florida. Playing the 510-yard 12th into the wind, I hit a 3-wood out of a fairway bunker 250 yards onto the green for an easy birdie. The shot caused a lot of commotion among my pals that day, Gary Player, Tom Weiskopf and Tony Jacklin, but I think if they'd looked at it a little more objectively—we had a few dollars riding on the game—they'd have been less impressed than they seemed to be. Sure it was a fine shot, but then everything was in my favor: firm sand with the ball sitting cleanly, a level lie and not much lip ahead of me. Under those circumstances getting distance from sand is not much more difficult than it is from the fairway.

2. In anything less than perfect conditions, your first thought when you find yourself in a fairway bunker should be position, not distance. Apply three rules in assessing what is feasible: (A) The more "cuppy" or buried the lie, the less cleanly the ball can be struck and the less far it can be hit. (B) The more angled or awkward your stance, the more you are likely to err in direction even though you may get good distance. (C) The higher the lip of the bunker ahead of you, the more lofted the club you must take to clear it and the less yardage it will produce. Given any or all of these conditions, figure out your best percentage recovery in terms of playing the next shot. With a severe lie and/or stance, the best percentage recovery for most players would be a sand-wedge blast out sideways. In a less severe situation, you might be able to get closer to the green by coming out obliquely with an 8- or 9-iron. Whatever you do, don't compound the original error into a major disaster.

3. Even when you feel you can go for all or most of the marbles, double-check what lies ahead before you do so. Give yourself as much margin for error as possible. For example, if there's a severe hazard such as water guarding the right side of the green and the pin is over that way, aim for the left side and rely on your putter. If there's big trouble between you and the green that you can't be sure of clearing unless you meet the ball perfectly, consider laying up. Remember, distance for its own sake might do something for your ego, but it can also do a lot of damage to your score. So, even when you think you can get distance from sand, use it intelligently.

4. You'll find it easier to meet the ball cleanly on a long sand shot if you move it back a little in your stance so that your hands stay well ahead of the clubface through impact. However, moving the ball back and keeping the hands in their normal address position has the effect of delofting the clubface, so adjust for that by using more loft than you would from the fairway—say a 5- or 6-iron instead of a 4-iron. Whatever club you use, remember to choke down on it a little to offset the effect of having lowered yourself in relation to the ball by digging your feet into the sand for a firm stance. One more tip: I find looking at the *top* rather than the back of the ball helps me to make cleaner contact on a long sand shot, especially when the lie is less than perfect.

5. What's to be done when you absolutely *have* to go for distance from a fluffy lie, as for example when a gamble is your only chance of staying alive in a head-to-head match? Probably the best tactic is what may best be described as a "cut blast" shot. Start by giving yourself a good solid stance by wiggling your feet firmly into the sand, and play the ball in your normal address position. Aim left to allow for the ball's left-to-right flight. Open the face of the club and swing it back slightly to the outside, making the fullest backswing you can without losing balance. Then hit as close behind the ball as the sand will permit, and as hard as you can with your right hand to keep your wrists from rolling over through impact and closing the clubface. This isn't an elegant stroke, but it can be played with just about any club except the driver or putter. With good execution, the ball will carry about two clubs less than from the fairway, i.e., a 5-iron "cut blast" will go about as far as a normal 7-iron shot.

Putting's as Important as the Full Swing

1. No matter how well you hit the ball from tee to green, your score won't reflect your shotmaking skills unless you also putt it in the hole in comparatively few strokes. On the other hand, no matter how badly you hit the ball through the air, by putting skillfully you'll always save something in terms of your overall score. Never lose sight of those two facts if you want to be a successful golfer. I've won a number of major championships when playing at considerably less than my best from tee to green, but I can't recall ever winning when driving and approaching well but putting really badly. That's one reason I built a practice green in my backyard—to encourage me to keep giving at least as much attention to my putting stroke as I do to my full swing.

2. If you believe you can get the ball into the hole or close, you generally will—and if you don't, you generally won't. That's why I think the No. 1 rule of putting must be to avoid all forms of negative thinking, especially the deep-seated feeling by some golfers that putting is not a rational part of golf's challenge. What I'm really saying is, don't begrudge this portion of the game—simply accept its special challenges as you do other aspects of the game. I promise you, the more positively you can approach the job mentally, the better you will putt—and score.

3. A big factor in being positive on the greens is having a clear mind about what you are trying to do with the ball. For that reason, I think it helps to decide whether you are by instinct or choice a "charge" or a "die" putter. The greatest charger in my time has been Arnold Palmer, who at his peak seemed to putt the ball so hard as to almost "trap" it into the hole. I'm much more of a "die" putter in that I prefer to ease the ball over the front lip, or, hopefully, have it topple in from its own weight if it catches a side rather than the meat of the hole. That's my instinctive way to putt, I guess, but it's also my conscious preference as being a lot easier on the nervous system than the charging technique —especially as one gets older.

4. Watch the finest putters in the game and you'll notice that all of them follow their own particular pattern of putting. If you don't already have such a procedure, I strongly advise you to develop one. Here are the elements I believe such a routine should include: (1) Time to study the grain, break and speed. Don't dawdle or procrastinate, but never hurry just to get a putt over with. (2) A positive plan based on that reading, in which the starting line of the putt and the force of the hit are clearly visualized. (3) A mental picture, derived from that plan, of the ball rolling over the green and dropping into the hole. (4) A setup and prestroking regimen that maximizes your physical feel for executing what you have mentally planned and visualized. (5) Some device to keep tension out of your muscles, such as a practice swing or two—rehearsals of the upcoming stroke. (6) The courage to stroke the ball only when you feel fully ready to do so.

5. There are all kinds of reasons—physique, age, strength, etc.—why you may not be able to get to the green in fewer than a certain number of strokes. But, assuming you are in good command of your basic faculties and have reasonable hand-eye coordination, there is no reason why you shouldn't learn to putt as well as any man or woman in history. Most professional tournaments today are won with about 120 putts for 72 holes, a per-round average of 30 or so. Determine your present standard by averaging your putts over your next 10 rounds. If you're around 30, go get some long-game lessons because you are definitely tour material on the greens. If you average 36 or just over, there is definite room for improvement, in your stroke, in your reading of greens or maybe in your attitude. If you're coming in at 40 or more, you need major surgery in all three.

How to Putt Better Before Reaching the Green

1. The best reason to learn to putt well is simply that you score better. But there's another reason, too, which is that the better you putt the less pressure you impose on your long game. Everyone who can play golf half decently has, I'm sure, been through those ugly cycles where the more often you three-putt or miss what seem makable putts, the closer you feel you have to hit the ball to the pin from the fairway, and therefore the farther down the fairway you have to drive it from the tee . . . and so on and on until, finally, you're pressing so hard on every shot that you couldn't break 90 even with Ben Hogan's swing. What's the answer to this kind of trauma? In my case, it's usually been found on the practice putting green rather than on the driving range—and frequently it takes a considerable amount of thought, work and perseverance.

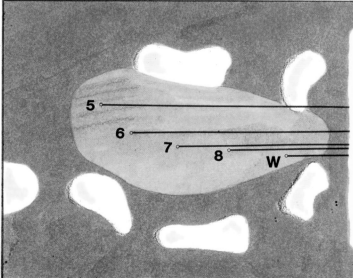

2. Many amateurs regularly place themselves in three-putt territory simply by neglecting to assess pin placement in relation to the depth of the green. Big greens—and particularly long greens—seem to be a feature of much modern course design, and they can make putting extremely demanding unless you pick the right clubs on approach shots. Pleasant Valley in Sutton, Mass., home of numerous PGA Tour events, is a classic example. The second green, a staggering 78 yards from front to back, calls for anything from a wedge to a 5-iron on the approach shot, and the 14th has required me to hit just about everything from a 6-iron to a 3-wood depending on the location of the pin. Those are exceptionally huge greens, but the point applies on many modern courses: club yourself poorly and you'll be working on a lot of monster putts.

4. Should you chip or putt from close to the green? The condition of the intervening surface must be the primary factor in that decision—the less close-cropped or smooth it is the less you can control a putted ball. Given decent ground conditions, a big factor becomes confidence. And common sense indicates that you should generally go with the stroke you think you can execute the best. In my case that usually means I'll reach for the putter because, putting so much more often than I chip, I figure I am bound to be better with that club.

3. The faster the greens the better I like them, so long as they are also smooth and true. This isn't because fast greens are easier to putt than slow ones—generally they are not—but rather because of the effect on the opposition. The tougher the conditions, the quicker they separate the wheat from the chaff, and the less chance luck or a hot streak will play a large role. The quicker the surface, the more careful I am on both full approach shots and recovery shots from just off the green to try to be putting uphill on my next stroke. It's my guess that more major championships have been lost on short downhill putts than by any other means. Conscious of that, I deliberately plan to avoid them on very fast greens, even to the point of preferring a breaking side-hiller to a straight putt down a sharp slope.

5. Quite often the first player to putt in a foursome will have the pin removed, and everyone else will automatically leave it out of the hole while they putt. By so doing, I believe, they often deprive themselves of a better target than the cup alone offers, even when it is fully and clearly visible. On almost all putts over, say, 25 feet, I find that leaving the pin in the hole definitely helps both my depth perception and my sense of aim and alignment, and you'll generally see Angelo tending it for me from that range. You'll also see him holding the pin whenever the hole is in a shadow or is otherwise difficult for me to see clearly.

Reading Greens

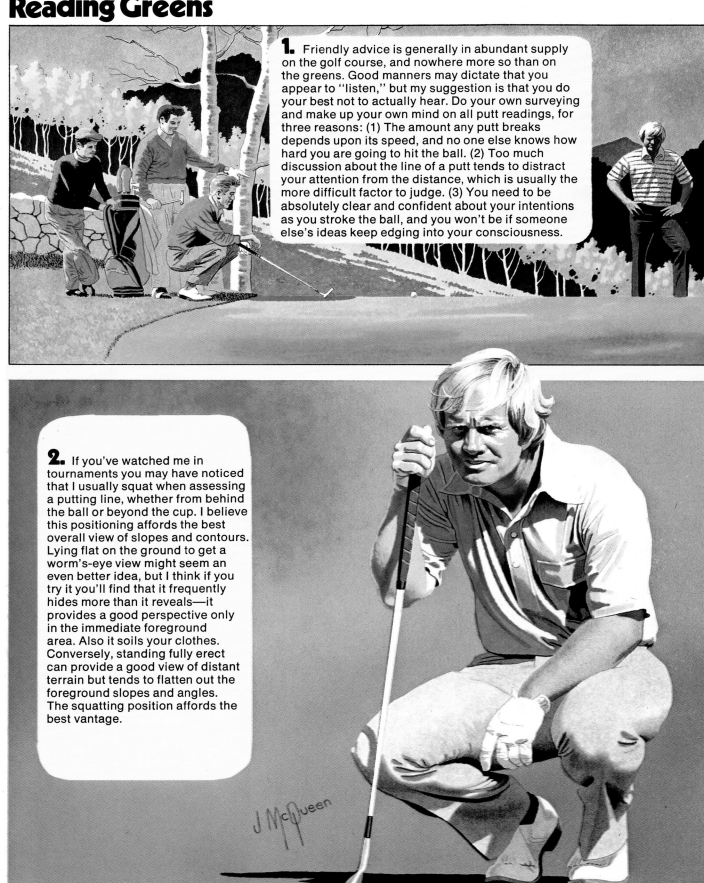

1. Friendly advice is generally in abundant supply on the golf course, and nowhere more so than on the greens. Good manners may dictate that you appear to "listen," but my suggestion is that you do your best not to actually hear. Do your own surveying and make up your own mind on all putt readings, for three reasons: (1) The amount any putt breaks depends upon its speed, and no one else knows how hard you are going to hit the ball. (2) Too much discussion about the line of a putt tends to distract your attention from the distance, which is usually the more difficult factor to judge. (3) You need to be absolutely clear and confident about your intentions as you stroke the ball, and you won't be if someone else's ideas keep edging into your consciousness.

2. If you've watched me in tournaments you may have noticed that I usually squat when assessing a putting line, whether from behind the ball or beyond the cup. I believe this positioning affords the best overall view of slopes and contours. Lying flat on the ground to get a worm's-eye view might seem an even better idea, but I think if you try it you'll find that it frequently hides more than it reveals—it provides a good perspective only in the immediate foreground area. Also it soils your clothes. Conversely, standing fully erect can provide a good view of distant terrain but tends to flatten out the foreground slopes and angles. The squatting position affords the best vantage.

J McQueen

3. Should you *always* study the line of a putt from both sides of the hole? Definitely not, would be my advice. If the view from behind the ball (which should always be your first assessment) tells you all you feel you need to know, then go ahead and play without further ado. That way you don't risk the drop in confidence you'd experience if the other view didn't exactly confirm your first impression. However, if you're in doubt after looking from behind the ball, the view from beyond the hole often will confirm or correct your first impression. If it doesn't, your last resort is to take a peek from the sides, looking particularly for rises or falls that you couldn't detect from front or back. In the interest of keeping play moving, do as much of your surveying as you possibly can while others are reading their putts—as you'll notice I do in tournament play.

ALWAYS

IF IN DOUBT

LAST RESORT

4. Be sure you know how to read the direction of grain and what to do about it. With most grasses, the grain is against you when the surface looks dull or dirty, and it is with you when it looks slick or shiny. For a further check, identify which way is west and the direction of drainage: grass generally grows toward the setting sun or with the nearest flow of water. Grain running against you slows down the ball, which necessitates firmer stroking. Conversely, grain running with you causes the ball to roll more freely, requiring a lighter touch. When the grain is across the line of a putt, the ball will veer in the direction of growth. It is particularly important on short cross-grain putts to assess and allow for the breaking effect of the grass if you plan to "die" the ball into the hole. On long putts across grain, be sure to allow for the ball's tendency to veer more and more with the grain as its forward momentum diminishes—especially when the ground also slopes in the direction of the grain. On *all* putts, recognize that the effects of grain increase as the grass gets longer late in the day. Aim and stroke accordingly.

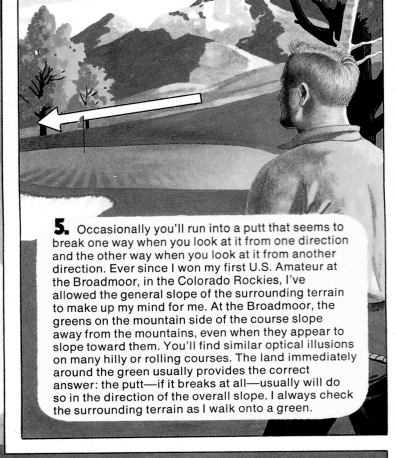

5. Occasionally you'll run into a putt that seems to break one way when you look at it from one direction and the other way when you look at it from another direction. Ever since I won my first U.S. Amateur at the Broadmoor, in the Colorado Rockies, I've allowed the general slope of the surrounding terrain to make up my mind for me. At the Broadmoor, the greens on the mountain side of the course slope away from the mountains, even when they appear to slope toward them. You'll find similar optical illusions on many hilly or rolling courses. The land immediately around the green usually provides the correct answer: the putt—if it breaks at all—usually will do so in the direction of the overall slope. I always check the surrounding terrain as I walk onto a green.

Lesson 26:
Long-Putt Tactics

1. Frequently in pro-ams, one of my amateur partners will walk up and hit a long putt after no more than a cursory glance at the territory he has to cover. He will then cuss or whine when the ball finishes many feet short, long or wide of the hole. Putting after just a casual glance at what lies between your ball and the cup may be OK if you're just out getting exercise, but it's a bad habit to get into if you're ever going to play golf seriously. The longer the putt, the greater the chance it will involve multiple breaks, or wet or dry spots, or variations in grass thickness, or changing grain patterns. All such conditions will affect the ball's behavior, which is one reason I frequently walk off very long putts, as well as assessing them from behind the ball and sometimes also from beyond the cup. Pacing the distance on a very long putt often helps me develop a feel for the "weight" of stroke I'll need to get it to the hole.

J. McQueen

2. Here are some further tactics that might help you on extremely long putts, as they have helped me over the years. First, take the most upright stance over the ball that you comfortably can, making it just that little bit easier to see the entire landscape between you and the hole and better judge the distance, right up to the moment of stroking. Next, concentrate more on solid contact with the ball than on pinpoint accuracy of line, because you are much more likely to be 10 feet short of the hole than 10 feet to the left or right on putts of this magnitude. Finally, don't be too greedy; from 50 feet or more you're doing well to get within three feet of the cup, so make that your target, not the hole itself. What I often do is visualize an imaginary circle around the cup about six feet in diameter and try to "die" the ball in the circle. That way I have a six-foot margin for error—three feet short and three feet long.

3. Occasionally on short putts I'll use a spot on the intended line as a target, but on longer putts I generally prefer to work with an overall picture of the line to be traveled rather than increase the pressure on myself by trying to hit a minute point on its route. However, where I have found putting to a particular mark or small area of green helpful is on double-breaking putts. Here's the technique. Study each break separately until you can identify the point at which you think the second break will begin to take effect. Then, in stroking, concentrate on getting the ball to that point by playing it to take the first break only. Obviously you also need to have programmed in a "weight" that will roll the ball the required distance.

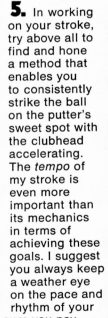

4. If you have trouble getting very long putts close, check your stroke as well as your green-reading techniques. Trying to *force* the putterhead to swing harder or faster to hit the ball farther is a sure way to misalign both its path and its face at impact. If you suspect you are doing this, take yourself off to the practice green and try controlling distance primarily through the length of your backswing rather than the force of the hit. I try to swing the putterhead at more or less the same pace on all putts—the ideal pace in my case being when I have a sense of the club virtually "swinging itself," rather than being forced or hurried in any way.

5. In working on your stroke, try above all to find and hone a method that enables you to consistently strike the ball on the putter's sweet spot with the clubhead accelerating. The *tempo* of my stroke is even more important than its mechanics in terms of achieving these goals. I suggest you always keep a weather eye on the pace and rhythm of your stroke. In reading greens, be sure you pay enough attention to the *speed* of long putts as well as to their line. Study your playing partners and I'm sure you'll notice that many more approach putts are left well short or hit way past the hole than are badly misdirected. Most people can intuitively "see" and remember the line of a putt better than they can compute and memorize its "weight." If you find you're among this group, then try putting with speed rather than line in the forefront of your mind.

Short-Putt Strategies

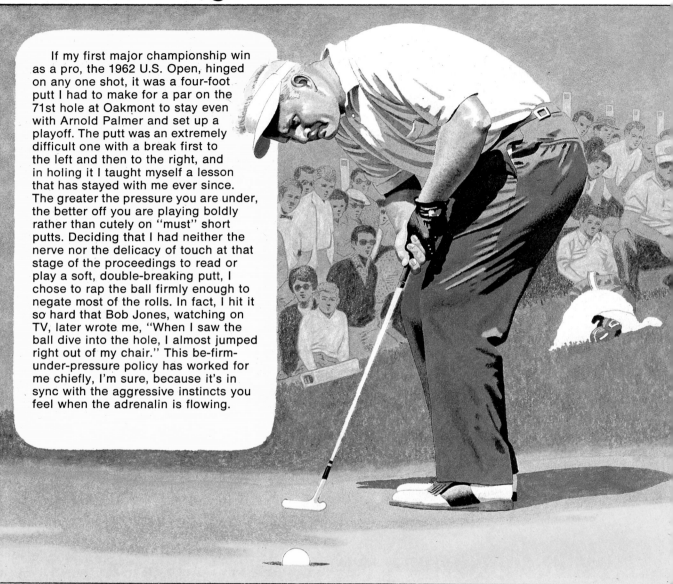

If my first major championship win as a pro, the 1962 U.S. Open, hinged on any one shot, it was a four-foot putt I had to make for a par on the 71st hole at Oakmont to stay even with Arnold Palmer and set up a playoff. The putt was an extremely difficult one with a break first to the left and then to the right, and in holing it I taught myself a lesson that has stayed with me ever since. The greater the pressure you are under, the better off you are playing boldly rather than cutely on "must" short putts. Deciding that I had neither the nerve nor the delicacy of touch at that stage of the proceedings to read or play a soft, double-breaking putt, I chose to rap the ball firmly enough to negate most of the rolls. In fact, I hit it so hard that Bob Jones, watching on TV, later wrote me, "When I saw the ball dive into the hole, I almost jumped right out of my chair." This be-firm-under-pressure policy has worked for me chiefly, I'm sure, because it's in sync with the aggressive instincts you feel when the adrenalin is flowing.

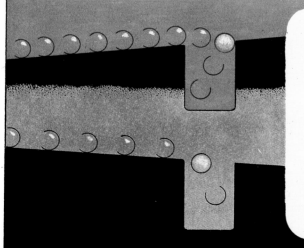

2. "Dying" the ball into the cup on a short, breaking putt requires that you perfectly judge both speed and direction, whereas by going more boldly for the hole you eliminate or reduce the subtleties involved. For that reason, when I am stroking the ball well—or under the kind of pressure I was at Oakmont—I'll almost always try to "firm" rather than "finesse" breaking *uphill* putts straight into the hole, or at least counter as much of the break as possible with speed. The raised rear portion of the cup offers more of a backstop than on a level putt—further encouragement to be bold. However, on short, breaking *downhill* putts my approach is exactly the opposite. Here I prefer to try to "die" the ball gently into the front of the hole after a careful computation of break and speed. One reason for that greater caution: the more downhill the putt, the less the lowered rear area of the cup serves as a backstop. The even bigger reason is that I hate having a longer putt coming back if I miss.

3. Although I'm not normally a "spot" putter, I have used the technique to good effect on shortish downhill putts, especially when they involve a fair amount of break. As an example, let's suppose I have a downhill 10-footer with a one-foot break. First, in assessing the downhill slope I'll decide how much force would be necessary to get the ball to the hole if the putt were level. Let's say it would require the speed of a level three-footer. Next, in assessing the break I'll identify a point say three feet along the curve to use as my target. Now, if I've judged both factors correctly, all I have to do is make the three-footer to make the 10-footer! It's never quite that easy, but I think you'll find this sort of "spotting" technique useful whenever it is difficult to get a complete impression of a putt's speed and break.

4. If you're missing too many short putts and suspect that misjudging the pace or the line is not the reason, look to your stroke. All of us tend to become a bit too tentative at times on the little ones, which frequently has the effect of causing clubhead deceleration before impact—a guaranteed way to leave the ball either short or wide of the hole. To get back on a firmer track, try making an exaggerated follow-through, swinging the putterhead six to nine inches directly along the line of the putt past the ball without letting its face close or open. A little practice doing this on three- and four-footers and you will quickly gain the feel of accelerating through the ball—not to mention that nice solid sensation of striking it with a truly square clubface.

5. You probably recognize that you feel more pressure often on the greens than anywhere else on a golf course. One salient reason is that your margin for error on a putt is less than on any other shot, but that's not the real throat-tightener in my view. Miss any other stroke in the game and you still have an opportunity to recover. Miss a short putt and you know it's irretrievable—a stroke gone forever. If the putt is *very* short, the prospect of the embarrassment you'll feel if you miss it often adds to the pressure.

What do you do about these emotions? Frankly, the only defense I know is the confidence born of acquired skill and previous success. And when that doesn't work? Well, my policy is to spend a minimum amount of psychic energy kicking myself and a maximum amount getting my mind onto what comes next. Sure, I needed that putt. Sure, I could have read it better, stroked it better, willed it into the hole harder. But life goes on. Here's another tee, another hole, another challenge. I try to do the only thing that really makes any sense in competitive terms: erase the past from my mind to make room for the present.

Some Special Putting Problems and Techniques

1. The odds are fairly long against your putter being the culprit if you have only spasmodic trouble on the greens, but if you become consistently inferior in this phase of the game, then a change of putter might provide at least a psychological boost. It could do more than that if the putter you've been using hasn't fully suited either your stroking style or the type of greens you normally play. If your natural or preferred putting motion is a long, flowing stroke, you'll probably be most comfortable and effective with a fairly heavy club and perhaps also with a longer-than-standard shaft. If you're more of a rap or tap putter, you'll likely do best with a medium-weight or even lighter club. Certainly, the faster the greens the more control a lot of good players feel they get from a reasonably light putter. If you're in doubt about your present putter, I suggest you ask your pro to let you try a few clubs from his rack—and have him look over your putting action, too.

Green speed, slopes and grain are the chief considerations in reading putts, but keep your mind alert to other, less obvious factors that can influence the ball's behavior. For instance, dew will have a slowing effect in the morning and evening, so look for most greens to be at their fastest around the middle of the day. Don't expect finely maintained fast greens to be greatly slowed by just a light shower that wets only the top surface—it usually takes a heavy soaking to really calm them down. Remember, especially in good weather, that the grass is growing as you play and that the greens will therefore become a little slower—and grainier—toward the final holes. Watch, too, for wind effect, especially on steep slopes and when a putt begins to lose momentum nearing the hole.

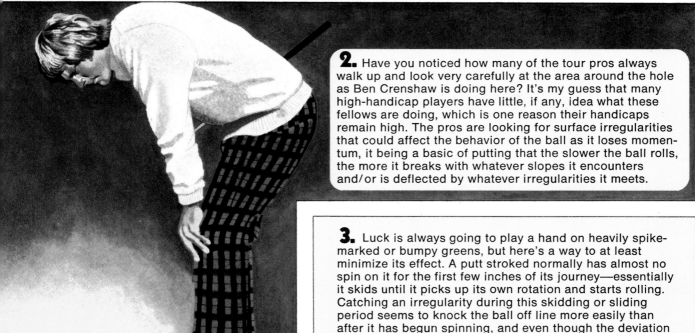

2. Have you noticed how many of the tour pros always walk up and look very carefully at the area around the hole as Ben Crenshaw is doing here? It's my guess that many high-handicap players have little, if any, idea what these fellows are doing, which is one reason their handicaps remain high. The pros are looking for surface irregularities that could affect the behavior of the ball as it loses momentum, it being a basic of putting that the slower the ball rolls, the more it breaks with whatever slopes it encounters and/or is deflected by whatever irregularities it meets.

3. Luck is always going to play a hand on heavily spike-marked or bumpy greens, but here's a way to at least minimize its effect. A putt stroked normally has almost no spin on it for the first few inches of its journey—essentially it skids until it picks up its own rotation and starts rolling. Catching an irregularity during this skidding or sliding period seems to knock the ball off line more easily than after it has begun spinning, and even though the deviation may be only a fraction of an inch at this point, it can become a couple of feet or more by the time the ball reaches the hole. With a little practice, you'll find you can ease, if not solve, this problem by meeting the ball slightly on the upswing. This will get the ball rolling more quickly, which helps negate any irregularities during those critical first few inches of travel.

4. Slightly varying how you work the clubface through the ball can help you cope with different green textures and speeds. For example, in 1972 I won seven times using three different types of impact. Early in the year I took the Doral-Eastern Open using an open-to-closed clubface motion through the ball because I felt that type of stroke would roll the ball most effectively along the top of spiky Bermuda greens. On the lightning fast greens of the U.S. Open at Pebble Beach I used the reverse action— a closed-to-open movement of the putter blade through the ball—because I felt it produced a softer contact. On the smooth, true, medium-paced greens of the Country Club of North Carolina for the PGA Match Play Championship, I was essentially a square-to-square putter, endeavoring never to let the clubface either open or close during the stroke.

J McQueen

Tailwinds, Headwinds and Crosswinds

1. You need intelligence and patience to play well in wind, but most of all you need a strong sense of realism and sure emotional control. Par climbs for *all* golfers along with wind force. For example, in a 10-mph breeze it may still be par 72, but in a 30-mph-or-more howler it could be 75 or 76. Build your overall scoring expectations, as well as your specific shotmaking strategies, around that fact. If you don't you'll quickly demoralize yourself into playing angrily or sloppily, or both.

NICKLAUS +5
JONES +7
SMITH +8

2. Many amateurs tend to relax their thought processes in a following wind, probably on the basis that it will help them achieve what always seems to be their chief golfing goal —distance. Don't make that mistake. Too much distance can be just as punitive as too little. Obviously a following wind makes it harder to stop the ball in the fairway or on the green, and you should club yourself and play accordingly. I naturally hit the ball high, but with a following wind I try to hit approach shots even higher—thereby seeking, in effect, the same kind of almost vertical descent I'd get on a windless day. To achieve the extra height and the steeper descent I take one or two clubs less than the distance would normally require and *hit hard.* Don't ever "baby" a shot when you want height—give it a good, solid whack.

3. How effectively you can cope with a strong headwind depends first on your ball-striking skills. If they are no better than average, then your primary goal in assessing and playing each shot should be safety, which means essentially staying away from the most severe trouble zones. If you are a fairly capable shotmaker, then your goal any time you're firing dead into a strong wind should be a low, boring flight in which the ball continues driving forward on a shallow parabola, rather than soaring to a peak, then dropping sharply. To minimize soaring you must minimize backspin, and you'll do that most effectively by playing the ball from right to left rather than straight or from left to right.

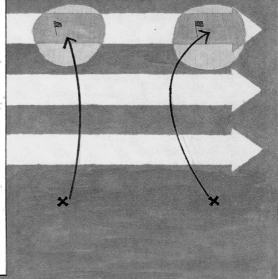

4. You have two options whenever the wind is fully or partially across the line of a shot. One is to try to "hold" the ball more or less straight by flighting it against the direction of the wind, i.e., drawing or hooking it into a wind from the left, and fading or slicing it into a wind from the right. The other option is simply to aim as much off the direct line as you think the wind will move the ball and play your normal shot, allowing the ball to be blown back to the target. I use both options depending on circumstances, plus at times a combination of both. The method you choose really depends on your shotmaking capabilities and your level of confidence at any given moment. If you can't consistently curve shots at will under ideal conditions, then I'd suggest you favor the second option.

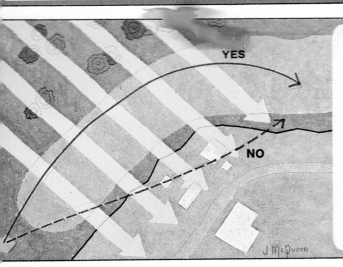

5. Even a severe wind can work for you on many occasions if you keep your eyes open and your wits intact. There's no better example than the 17th at the Old Course of St. Andrews, the famous Road Hole. This is a long par 4 on which the fairway swings to the right about 220 yards from the tee. The ideal driving line on a calm day is over the forecourt of the hotel, thereby cutting the corner of the dogleg. But that involves flirting with out-of-bounds—a particularly dangerous line when there is left-to-right wind. In such conditions the intelligent golfer who hits down the *left* side of the fairway either straight or with a little fade benefits from the wind in three ways: (1) He minimizes the risk of going OB; (2) he reduces the chance of finding the heavy left rough if a draw turns into a hook, and (3) the wind will add many yards to the drive as it bends it to the right.

How to Cope with Wind on Tee Shots

1. You need every advantage you can muster playing in the wind, and there's no better place to start strategizing than on the tee. In a crosswind most weekend golfers, if they don't let their egos or emotions get in the way, will choose to aim off to one side and let the wind blow the ball back on target, rather than try to fight the wind by curving the ball against it. In that case, if the wind is from left to right, setting up as far as possible to the *left* side of the tee and aiming down the left side gives you the maximum amount of fairway to play with. Conversely, of course, you get more driving area when the wind is from the right by teeing up as far to the *right* as possible and aiming down the right side of the fairway.

2. As you undoubtedly know from experience, the more loft on the club the less likely you are to hook or slice badly. Take advantage of that fact on downwind tee shots. The breezes are going to give you extra yardage anyway, so you don't always have to beat on the ball with the biggest club in your bag. If your driver tends to do you injury, or hazards make accuracy imperative, use your 3-wood or an even more lofted club. However, don't let the lesser firepower in your hands cause you to subconsciously ease up on the shot. To take full advantage of the wind you need to get the ball well up in the air, so make a good, full, firm swing, and *release* through impact. Don't let the wind lure you into "steering" your shots—a definite danger in rough conditions.

NO

YES

3. Should you tee the ball lower hitting directly into the wind? This sometimes is advocated for a lower flight, but I don't agree. First, the lower the ball is teed the more downward blow it encourages, and the more downward the blow the greater the backspin, and the greater the backspin the more the ball will soar. Second, many golfers will involuntarily open the face of a driver through impact when the ball is teed low in an instinctive effort to get it airborne, which produces the one thing you don't want: height (not to mention a slice or push). Third, if there's any time you really need a solid hit it's driving into a high wind. You have a better chance for a flush impact if you get all the clubface on the back of the ball. So my advice is to tee the ball at normal height, headwind or no.

4. Perhaps the toughest hole in championship golf to figure out in any kind of wind is No. 12 at Augusta National. It's only 155 yards, but many a Masters has been lost right there. The narrow, diagonally angled green with Rae's Creek in front and sloping bunkers and a rough bank behind are worrisome factors. But the most frightening consideration is what will happen to the tee shot when it climbs above the thick stand of trees sheltering the right side of the tee and beyond. The best clue is to carefully study which way and how forcibly the tops of the trees are blowing, and this is a tactic most experienced tour players use on *all* drives and approach shots on wooded courses in windy weather. You'll receive fewer unpleasant surprises if you make a habit of doing the same.

5. To me, the toughest of all winds is a following wind that also quarters from left to right. This type of wind prompts many golfers to make a special effort to keep the head and upper body well behind the ball through impact. However, if you are not careful this effort can in turn promote a tendency to sway rather than coil on the backswing, and it also can inhibit your leg and hip action through the ball. The best defense against both these dangers is simply to be aware of them, perhaps to the point of consciously prefacing each swing with the thought to turn fully and clear fully.

NO **YES**

J McQueen

Approaching and Putting When the Wind is Strong

1. Wind affects more than your swing and the way the ball behaves in the air. Ground conditions change, too, in ways that demand special alertness and care in planning, especially drives to angled or sloping fairways and all approach shots. Wind quickly dries out both the top surface of the ground and the grass itself, making for greatly increased bounce and roll no matter how finely you flight and spin the ball. Frequently after a day or two—or even an hour or two—of gusty conditions a tee shot that would normally stop in the fairway will run through a dogleg or kick off a slope into trouble. Approach shots present even greater challenges, calling at the planning stage for safety ahead of all other factors.

2. Obviously, the easiest way to keep the ball down when the wind is against you is to use less-lofted clubs for approach shots, and anyone who hopes to be a good wind player should definitely learn the tactics and techniques involved by actually practicing them in rough conditions. Frequently in a strong blow I'll drop down not just one club but *two*. For instance, if the shot is 7-iron distance under normal conditions but I'm leaning into a strong wind, I'll take a 5-iron and either choke down or swing easily. You should learn to do this with all the irons, but it is imperative with the pitching clubs where excessive height often equals disaster. For example, if you're wedge distance from the cup, play either a three-quarter shot with a 9-iron or a half-shot with an 8. Also, look for opportunities to pitch and run the ball rather than trying to fly it all the way to the pin.

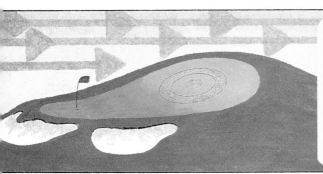

3. With a tight pin position and a really strong following wind, it sometimes becomes impossible to shoot for the flag and still stay on the green. In that case, don't try. Instead, aim for the fattest part of the green and rely on your putter. Also, learn to analyze and use slopes. For instance, if the pin is to the left but the right portion of the green rises in back and also slopes left, then a ball hit into this area will stop more quickly and will bounce and roll in the general direction of the hole. Also, if you possess the shotmaking skills, don't overlook the stoppage effects of fading into ground sloping left and drawing into ground sloping right.

4. Maintaining balance is always tough in a really strong wind. One way to anchor yourself more firmly is to widen your stance, but this has the effect of reducing your body turn and shortening your backswing. Generally, you'll lose a little distance when that happens, so be sure to take plenty of club. One way to still gain maximum distance from a more compact swing—for the capable shotmaker, at least—is to counter the reduced body turn with extra hand action. Thus, in certain wind conditions, I'll often simply relax my wrists and allow them to cock a little earlier going back, which has the effect of producing a more lively release through the ball.

5. A really strong wind, particularly on an exposed course, will affect even a rolling ball, so don't drop your guard once you get close to or on the green. Remember when chipping or approach-putting that a crosswind will either increase or diminish the amount the ball breaks, especially as it loses speed. In chipping, play generally for roll rather than flight, but don't overlook the possible "stopping" power of a headwind on a lofted shot when you have little green to work with.
In making the stroke, anchor yourself to the ground as solidly as you can, keep your head still, and strike the ball smoothly but *positively*—accelerate the clubhead through it. Remember that any hesitancy in the stroke will cause clubhead deviation at impact and that the resulting misdirection generally will be increased by a strong wind.

Lesson 32:
Wet-Weather Strategies

1. As with all difficult conditions, playing in rain or on wet ground requires first an internal pep talk regarding attitude and goals. If there's nothing you can do about the conditions, then the more you can accept them as interesting challenges, the better you'll cope with them. Conversely, the more you let them get to you emotionally, the poorer will be your patience, your reasoning powers and your ability to concentrate on the specifics of shotmaking. So be a fatalist—and also a realist. You probably won't play and score as well as you might under ideal conditions—but the odds are that no one else will, either. Keeping that thought in mind in rough weather has helped me win a lot of tournaments.

2. One of your best aids in sloppy weather is a clear understanding of the rules relating to casual water. The Rules of Golf define it: "Casual water is any temporary accumulation of water which is visible before or after the player takes his stance and which is not a hazard of itself or is not in a water hazard. Snow and ice are either casual water or loose impediments, at the option of the player." Under Rule 32 you can obtain relief from casual water, without penalty, anywhere on the golf course, by lifting and dropping the ball on drier ground, so long as you don't drop it closer to the hole, or, if you're in a hazard, outside that hazard. Also, you can *clean* the ball when you lift it.

3. Golf is a game of spin, and when water comes between clubface and ball at impact the amount of spin imparted to the ball—both backspin and sidespin—is diminished. Learn to allow for that on all your shots. The wetter the conditions the lower and longer your approach shots will tend to fly and the faster they'll land, so consider using a club that will give you more loft than normally—a 4-wood instead of a 2-iron, for example. Similarly, the more that water or wet grass gets between club and ball, the tougher it becomes to fade or draw consistently.

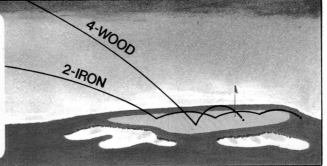

4. The sloppier the conditions, the tougher it is to keep a solid footing. Wearing shoes with a complete set of good spikes makes the job easier, but only if you keep them free of mud and grass. Use the point of a tee or a pitch repair tool to scrape away the gook at least before every drive and preferably before every shot in really bad conditions. If the ground is so slippery that there is no way to be sure of firm footing, then take more club and make a slower and easier swing.

5. Hitting down on the ball reduces the effective loft of the club, which, as we've just seen, is the last thing you want when playing from wet turf. Therefore, the more cleanly you can sweep the ball with all the clubs, the better your scoring chances. Prime requirement for picking the ball cleanly is meeting it at the exact bottom of the swing arc. This usually involves moving the ball a little farther forward in relation to the feet at address. Experiment in practice to find your best wet-weather ball location.

6. Although it's more difficult to curve the ball in the wet, the really good "mudders" on tour will frequently play a type of approach shot that largely counteracts the ball's tendency to fly lower and land harder. This is a hard-hit fade, using one club less than would usually be required. Keys to the shot are aligning left of target with the clubface square or slightly open, ball forward, and a strong arm swing with very little hand action through impact to prevent the clubface from closing.

Lesson 33:

"Smell the Flowers" and Play Better Golf

1. Ever notice that many amateurs—and even some tour golfers—play better after a layoff? One reason is rekindled interest in the game. Too much golf can make anyone stale, which is why I've always tried to pace myself so carefully throughout my career. Another reason, and one often overlooked, is that a more relaxed approach to the game comes from not expecting too much of yourself. Play and practice a great deal and you'll tend to set high targets; stay away from golf for awhile and you don't demand as much of yourself when you first tee it up again. You are more relaxed both physically and mentally, and often you play better. I'm not suggesting that your game will improve if you only play once a month, but what I am recommending is that you allow yourself to relax both mentally and physically as much as possible when you do play. The opposite to relaxation is tension, and the more physically tense you are, the less effectively you'll swing the club. Accepting reality is the No. 1 prerequisite to staying fairly loose. If your handicap is 12, don't expect to break 80 every time you go out. Also, don't expect never to make mistakes. I count myself lucky if I hit six shots a round exactly as I've planned them. Finally, don't berate yourself when you do make a mistake—get your mind out of the past and onto the recovery.

2. Probably the loosest of all the game's greats was Walter Hagen, and I believe his most famous line —"Don't forget to stop and smell the flowers along the way"—offers a good lesson about relaxation to all golfers. Of the four or so hours it takes you to play a round, if you're an 85-shooter, say, you actually need to focus all of your mental faculties on the game for perhaps a quarter of that time, and apply yourself physically for, at most, 15 minutes. By allowing yourself to "smell the flowers" the rest of the time, you not only relax but also refresh the mind and muscles for their next burst of activity. Remember, no one can fix and hold his mind on a single subject for as long as it takes to play 18 holes.

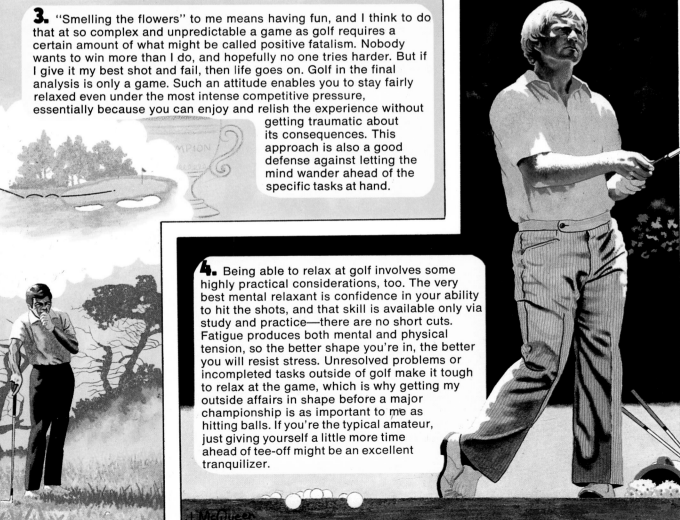

3. "Smelling the flowers" to me means having fun, and I think to do that at so complex and unpredictable a game as golf requires a certain amount of what might be called positive fatalism. Nobody wants to win more than I do, and hopefully no one tries harder. But if I give it my best shot and fail, then life goes on. Golf in the final analysis is only a game. Such an attitude enables you to stay fairly relaxed even under the most intense competitive pressure, essentially because you can enjoy and relish the experience without getting traumatic about its consequences. This approach is also a good defense against letting the mind wander ahead of the specific tasks at hand.

4. Being able to relax at golf involves some highly practical considerations, too. The very best mental relaxant is confidence in your ability to hit the shots, and that skill is available only via study and practice—there are no short cuts. Fatigue produces both mental and physical tension, so the better shape you're in, the better you will resist stress. Unresolved problems or incompleted tasks outside of golf make it tough to relax at the game, which is why getting my outside affairs in shape before a major championship is as important to me as hitting balls. If you're the typical amateur, just giving yourself a little more time ahead of tee-off might be an excellent tranquilizer.

J McQueen

Lesson 34:
Pitching and Chipping Ploys

1. Most pitches and chips are recovery shots, and all recovery shots require first an acceptance that you've made a mistake or got an unlucky bounce and then an immediate deletion of that fact from your mind. What just happened is history, and there's nothing you can do about it. What you're confronted with now is the present, and the more exclusively your mind focuses on it the better you'll deal with it. Don't compound the error (or the tough break, if you prefer). In the situation illustrated here the first thought of many handicap players would probably be how to get close to the hole. My first thought would be getting the ball somewhere on the green so I could two-putt at worst and move on with my hide still fairly intact. In other words—as these pages have continually emphasized—be REALISTIC in all your shot planning.

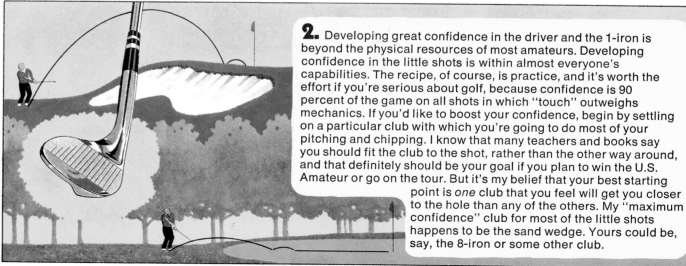

2. Developing great confidence in the driver and the 1-iron is beyond the physical resources of most amateurs. Developing confidence in the little shots is within almost everyone's capabilities. The recipe, of course, is practice, and it's worth the effort if you're serious about golf, because confidence is 90 percent of the game on all shots in which "touch" outweighs mechanics. If you'd like to boost your confidence, begin by settling on a particular club with which you're going to do most of your pitching and chipping. I know that many teachers and books say you should fit the club to the shot, rather than the other way around, and that definitely should be your goal if you plan to win the U.S. Amateur or go on the tour. But it's my belief that your best starting point is *one* club that you feel will get you closer to the hole than any of the others. My "maximum confidence" club for most of the little shots happens to be the sand wedge. Yours could be, say, the 8-iron or some other club.

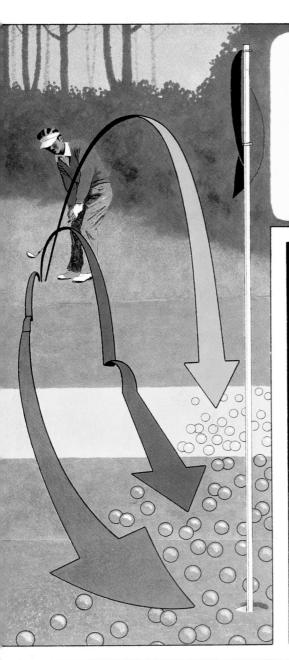

3. You might notably improve your pitching and chipping by conducting a little experiment to determine which is your best *natural* route to the hole from the routine greenside situation. The options are: primarily through the air, chiefly along the ground, or roughly half and half of both. Again, the highly skilled player can elect any of these routes, depending on the lie and the terrain, but for the weekender this may be asking too much. Most golfers—even the tour players—have a preference between flight and roll, both in visualizing and playing these little shots. To identify your most natural route, play 20 shots using your favorite club and trying to loft the ball most of the way to the hole from just off the green, then 20 more trying to run it mainly along the ground, then 20 trying for equidistant flight and roll. The batch of balls that finishes the closest tells you the type of shot to prefer.

4. If you've watched the pros much, you might have noticed that many of them rarely take a practice swing before a drive or long approach shot, but they almost always take a goodly number of practice swings before any little pitch or chip shot such as Hubert Green is facing here. Observe carefully and you'll further note that the more tricky the pitch or chip, the more practice swings are taken. Why? The good player's full swing is sufficiently "grooved" that it rarely needs rehearsing. However, when the swing is to be anything less than full, it needs ample rehearsing to "fit" its length and force to the distance to be covered, and to implant a "picture" of the required action in the mind and muscles. Your short game will benefit from similar complete rehearsals.

5. You wouldn't stroke a putt before looking over the terrain to be covered—the pitch or the chip should get like consideration. In "reading" these shots your first objective will usually be getting the ball as close to the cup as *realistically* possible, but take into account what you'll have left if you don't lay it dead. For example, the tendency on pitch shots, because you necessarily swing more uprightly with the short irons, is to impart a little cut spin to the ball, causing it to break right on landing. Thus if the pin is located as illustrated here, the intelligent shot would be to insure against the ball's break—and a subsequent very long and tricky putt—by playing a few feet to the left. In chipping, or whenever the ball will roll extensively, take into account grain, contours and turf condition as much as when putting. Try to leave yourself putts that are straight and either level or slightly uphill. In other words, keep on playing the percentages.

Maneuvering the Ball

1. Most good golfers rarely try to hit longer shots dead straight. They prefer to spin the ball either slightly from left to right or from right to left. Being able to repeat one or the other "shape" consistently breeds confidence, so intelligent players go with their preferred pattern whenever possible because it's the high-percentage shot. Another reason also involves percentages, as these two drawings illustrate. The first shows how a primarily left-to-right player, like myself, plays a routine approach shot. Let's say I plan to fade the ball 15 feet. If I'm spot on, I'm in the hole (assuming perfect distance). If I inadvertently hit the ball dead straight, I have a 15-foot putt. If I double the amount of fade I've planned, I still have a 15-foot putt. Now look at the second drawing for a golfer who tries to hit the ball dead straight. If he executes perfectly, super. However, if he cuts the shot only as much as I did when overdoing my fade, he has a 30-foot putt. If he pulls the ball straight left, chances are he'll again have a longer putt than I have. Assuming equally faulty execution through 18 holes, the controlled left-to-right or right-to-left player is going to be putting from something like half the distance of the go-straight-for-it golfer.

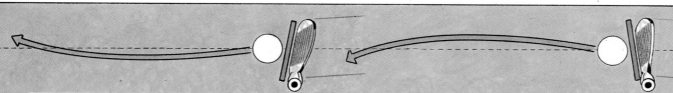

2. To learn how to consistently fade or draw the ball, it helps first to clearly understand the differences between these shots and their ugly sisters—the slice and the hook—plus what causes these differences. In a fade the ball starts *slightly* left of or straight along the target line and curves *slightly* right of that path toward the end of its flight. The draw is the opposite of that pattern: a starting path along or *slightly* right of the target line and a *slight* curve to the left toward the end of the trajectory. A slice or a hook is simply much larger—and usually much more punishing—than a fade or draw. How do they get that way? The answer lies in the interaction of the clubhead path and clubface angle at impact. Any time the clubface looks to the right of where the clubhead is swinging, the ball will be spun to the right; and any time the clubface looks left of the clubhead's direction, the ball will be spun to the left. The ball curves only slightly in a fade or draw because these angles mismatch only minimally. The greater the mismatching, the more the ball curves. So, to turn a slice or hook into a fade or draw, the primary area for work is always your clubhead/clubface interaction at impact.

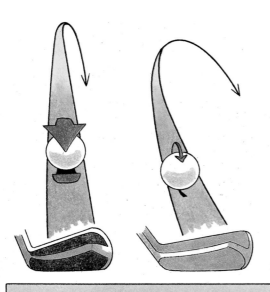

3. Now let me add a qualifier to the foregoing. If you watch top golfers carefully, you will notice that the shorter the shot the less they curve the ball. Also, if you care to analyze your own game, you will almost certainly discover that you, too, slice or hook progressively less the shorter your shots —although you still may often miss the target by pulling or pushing the ball. The reason for all this is built into your golf clubs. To explain it simply, the more loft a club possesses the greater the backspin it imparts, and the greater the backspin the ball carries the more resistant it is to the effects of sidespin. Thus, the more lofted the club, the less the ball can be curved in flight; the shorter the shot, the more directly to the target you should set up and swing. And those pulls and pushes? With little, if any, sideway curve on the ball, these are true reflections of your swing path through impact—and thus a sure indicator of what you most need to work on in practice.

4. There are two ways to intentionally fade or draw the ball with the longer clubs. One is to change your grip and swing path, moving your hands farther to the left and swinging from out to in for a fade, or turning your hands more to the right and swinging from in to out for a draw. Use these techniques if they work consistently well for you. But if they don't, try my method—a much simpler one, I believe. To fade a shot, leave your grip alone but open the clubface slightly at address, align yourself a little left of target, then swing normally. To draw a shot, reverse the procedure: grip as usual, close the clubface slightly and align your body a little right of target. These adjustments allow maximum shot-curving potential for minimal disruption of playing patterns and "feels." But a word of warning: swinging normally in both cases means swinging so that your clubhead path on the takeaway and at impact matches your body alignment, *not* your direct ball-to-target line.

5. Here are three tips that will further help you curve the ball. First, match your waggle to the swing path that will produce your desired curvature, i.e., from out-to-in for a fade and in-to-out for a draw. Second, in practice, work on matching your hip clearance to your intended flight path, unwinding quickly but *smoothly* for a fade to help keep the clubface open through the ball, and less quickly when you want your hands and arms to roll it closed to produce a draw. Third, seek the feeling of matching your hand-and-wrist release to your desired flight pattern, delaying the roll of the right forearm over the left for a fade, and allowing your hands and arms to release as quickly as possible for a draw.

Finessing the Ball for Lower Scores

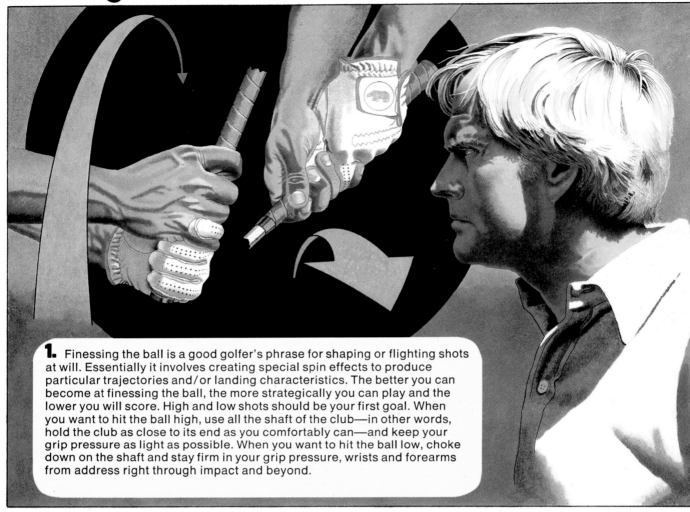

1. Finessing the ball is a good golfer's phrase for shaping or flighting shots at will. Essentially it involves creating special spin effects to produce particular trajectories and/or landing characteristics. The better you can become at finessing the ball, the more strategically you can play and the lower you will score. High and low shots should be your first goal. When you want to hit the ball high, use all the shaft of the club—in other words, hold the club as close to its end as you comfortably can—and keep your grip pressure as light as possible. When you want to hit the ball low, choke down on the shaft and stay firm in your grip pressure, wrists and forearms from address right through impact and beyond.

2. The ability to hit the ball high and thereby stop it quickly has been perhaps my greatest single golfing asset over the years, especially in major championships where much long-iron play is called for and greens tend to be firm and fast. Height comes from backspin, which comes from maximum use of the loft built into the clubface, which in turn comes from a full, free release of the clubhead through the ball without the face closing. You should set up at address to promote these impact ingredients. Play the ball as far forward in your stance as you comfortably can and open the clubface. In aiming, allow for a left-to-right flight. Then, using light grip pressure and relaxed wrists to help you do so, be sure to really *release* the clubhead—even to the point of feeling you are flinging or slinging it through the ball. Work on this action in practice before you try it under pressure on the course. Try for the feeling that your right hand is staying *under* your left until the ball is well on its way. Use this technique only from decent lies—it's extremely difficult when the ball is sitting "tight."

3. Even good golfers find it tough to hit the ball both very low and reasonably straight, the tendency generally being to hook or pull-hook. However, learning to reduce height by "driving" the ball more directly forward, rather than upward, is within the capability of anyone who breaks 90 regularly. Such shots are useful when hitting into wind, in playing beneath tree limbs and when you need extra roll for maximum distance. Set up to the shot at address by moving the ball back in your stance with your hands well ahead of the ball and the clubface square or slightly closed. These adjustments have the effect of delofting the clubface, and the object in swinging is to keep it that way through impact. A firm grip will help you do so, as will the feeling of keeping the back of your left hand well ahead of the ball until well beyond impact. On this shot it's essential to unwind the hips in good time to make way for the arms to swing freely past the body. If they don't, your wrists will flip the clubhead in too early and you'll get too much height—and probably in a left-to-left direction. Practice the technique before you try it in play, and allow for more draw or hook the less lofted the club.

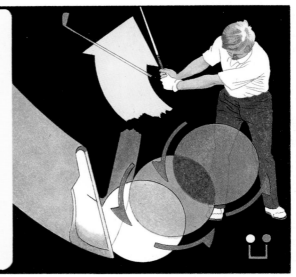

4. There are many times in golf where extra "bite" is useful—or even imperative. The only way to achieve this is by imparting additional backspin to the ball, which creates extra height and thus a steeper angle of descent, plus more "grab" on landing. Goal No. 1 for maximum backspin is a very clean hit—i.e., ball before grass or ground—and the easiest way to achieve this is to steepen the angle at which the clubface meets the ball. The good player often will do this simply by moving the ball back a little at address and swinging more uprightly, perhaps by bringing the wrists into play a little earlier going back. Try this technique yourself in practice, but if it's too tough, then get your extra bite from the fade—a shot that automatically creates a steeper angle of hit and thus a higher trajectory. Simply open the clubface at address, aim yourself left of target, then swing normally. When the ground is hard, allow for the ball to hop and run from left to right as well as curving that way in the air.

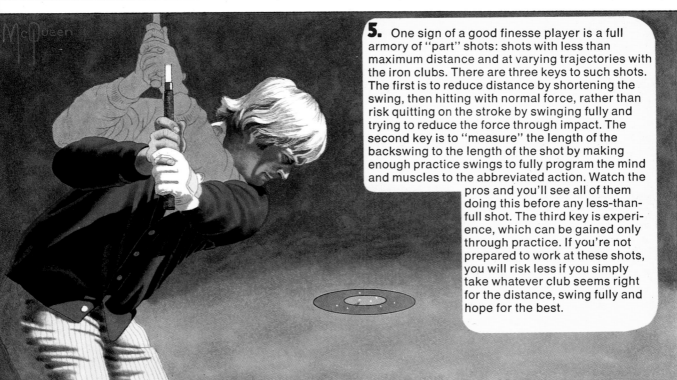

5. One sign of a good finesse player is a full armory of "part" shots: shots with less than maximum distance and at varying trajectories with the iron clubs. There are three keys to such shots. The first is to reduce distance by shortening the swing, then hitting with normal force, rather than risk quitting on the stroke by swinging fully and trying to reduce the force through impact. The second key is to "measure" the length of the backswing to the length of the shot by making enough practice swings to fully program the mind and muscles to the abbreviated action. Watch the pros and you'll see all of them doing this before any less-than-full shot. The third key is experience, which can be gained only through practice. If you're not prepared to work at these shots, you will risk less if you simply take whatever club seems right for the distance, swing fully and hope for the best.

Escaping from the Tall Grass

1. A player's behavior when in trouble is one of the key differences between golf's great winners and many of the outstanding ball-strikers who have failed to build records commensurate with their physical talents. I'd guess that all great champions, sooner or later, have been able to recognize and obey the first law of playing *all* trouble shots: STAY COOL. The sharper your mental faculties when confronting a problem, the better your chances of solving it. Try to be philosophical about both the nature of the game and your own frailties. You are *always* going to get unlucky breaks and you are *always* going to make mistakes. Forget them as soon as they happen—they are history. Concentrate on *now* to the exclusion of all else—then, if the mistakes were yours rather than the golf course's, reflect and work on them later on the practice tee. I can't help you develop a winning mental attitude, but I can show you some recovery techniques, and we'll cover them in this and the next four articles.

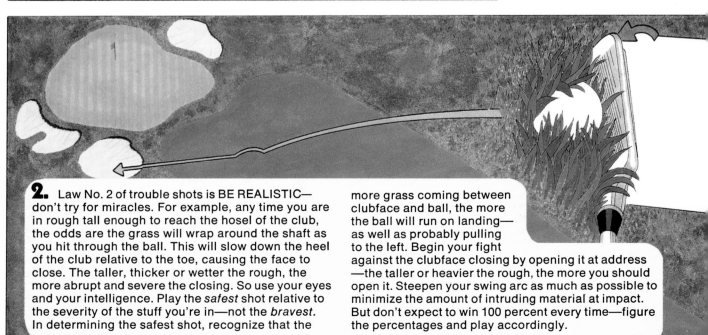

2. Law No. 2 of trouble shots is BE REALISTIC—don't try for miracles. For example, any time you are in rough tall enough to reach the hosel of the club, the odds are the grass will wrap around the shaft as you hit through the ball. This will slow down the heel of the club relative to the toe, causing the face to close. The taller, thicker or wetter the rough, the more abrupt and severe the closing. So use your eyes and your intelligence. Play the *safest* shot relative to the severity of the stuff you're in—not the *bravest*. In determining the safest shot, recognize that the more grass coming between clubface and ball, the more the ball will run on landing—as well as probably pulling to the left. Begin your fight against the clubface closing by opening it at address—the taller or heavier the rough, the more you should open it. Steepen your swing arc as much as possible to minimize the amount of intruding material at impact. But don't expect to win 100 percent every time—figure the percentages and play accordingly.

3. Even when it doesn't reach up to the hosel, long, wet or fluffy grass presents a problem, in the form of the "flier" lie, the most common trouble shot in the game. You encounter it when just missing fairways, or when fairways are shaggy or thick with clover, or in hollows or pockets that the mowers haven't been able to cut close. The challenge is to allow a minimum amount of grass to intrude between clubface and ball at impact, and the way to achieve this is with a steeper swing arc and a high, fading, soft-landing shot. However, if there's no way to be certain of avoiding a flier, allow for it in your shot strategy. For example, if you are 5-iron distance

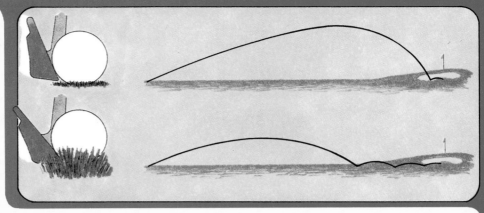

from a green with little trouble in front but severe problems behind, play a 6- or 7-iron. If the ball then flies and rolls "hot," chances are it will reach the putting surface. If it flies and rolls normally, you are left with an easy pitch or chip from the fairway.

J. McQueen

4. In analyzing any shot from rough, don't overlook the direction in which the grass inclines in deciding your strategy. The more the grass grows or angles toward the target, the "hotter" the ball will fly and roll, so club yourself accordingly. Grass growing or inclining away from the target will be more resistant, reducing the distance of the shot, so be sure to give yourself plenty of club. When the grass is severely inclined either away from or toward the target there is a tendency for it to nose the ball downward at impact, so make a special effort to get the clubhead well *under the* ball through impact.

5. Imagination is a great weapon against golfing adversity. When surveying any trouble shot, I try to let my mind run freely through the gamut of possible recovery techniques that I've learned through experience. Many are quickly eliminated as impossible or impractical, but usually I end up with two or three alternatives. Then, to check their feasibility, I use my imagination to fully visualize how the ball would likely behave in each instance. If I can't honestly "see" the shot behaving as I'd like it to, then I know my chances of executing it are slim indeed. Try this technique the next time you're just about to attempt a 3-wood off a sidehill lie out of deep, wet rough to a small green with a lake in front. Stop a moment and visualize what is *really* likely to happen if you attempt such a shot. It's my guess that the nasty pictures you get will quickly change your mind.

Hitting Long and Short from the Rough

1. The amateur's best friends when a long way from home in light or moderate rough are almost always the fairway woods, especially the 4, 5 and up. These clubs have bigger and more smoothly rounded heads that enable them to cut through long grass more readily than the longer irons and deviate less in face alignment as they do so. Also, by flying the ball high they will produce a softer-landing shot than is normally possible with a long iron when grass intervenes between its face and the ball at impact. You can further increase height, and thus stopping power, by applying some cut action to the ball. Play the ball back a little in your stance, aim left, open the clubface, be sure to lead the downswing with your legs and hips, hit sharply down into the ball, and allow for a fade. Remember that, by choking down on the club, you can use this shot for considerably less distance than the full potential of the club. Consider it for approaches from shaggy or soggy fairways, as well as from light or moderate rough.

2. Getting distance *and* height from really heavy or matted rough is usually impossible. So is getting distance *and* pinpoint accuracy. However, there is a way to advance the ball considerably from some types of tall grass, so long as you don't have to stop it quickly or place it precisely. This technique becomes a useful tactic on a par 5 or long par 4 following an errant drive when there isn't too much trouble up ahead. To play the shot, take a club with a reasonable amount of loft—say a 4- or 5-iron —and move the ball back in your stance as far as you comfortably can, with your hands set well ahead of it and the clubface square or even slightly hooded at address. Then grip firmly, make a good turn, and—leading always with your left hand—punch the clubhead down into the back of the ball as hard and abruptly as you can. This is not an elegant stroke so don't concern yourself too much with form—make "hit the daylights out of it" your primary thought. The result won't look elegant, either—usually a low, squirting shot with a good deal of hook—but, used intelligently, it could very well help you salvage a par or better.

3. One of the most common trouble shots in golf is the short pitch from rough around the green. Often the ball has to be made to carry some sort of obstacle, such as a bunker or water hazard, and frequently it must also be made to stop quickly, either to get within possible one-putt range or, in some cases, simply to hold the green. When the rough is not too severe and/or the ball is lying fairly well (i.e., with a reasonable cushion of grass beneath it), forget about trying to impart heavy backspin and play a lob shot or "floater." Select a pitching wedge or sand wedge, use all the shaft, move the ball well forward in your stance, open the clubface a little at address, and make a smooth, firm-wristed, almost slow-motion backswing, using mostly your arms. Coming down, try to retain the same overall slow-motion pace of arm swing while sliding the clubface firmly beneath the ball without any sudden or severe wrist flipping. Feel that your right hand is delivering the clubface very deliberately under and through the ball without overtaking or crossing over your left hand. And look hard at the

back of the ball throughout the stroke. Properly played, the ball will float out slow and high and land softly with very little roll. Adjust the distance by the length of the arm swing, rather than by accelerating the clubhead with your hands and wrists through impact.

4. When the rough is heavy or wet and the ball lies well down in it, you face a much sterner challenge and should beware of becoming overambitious. Simply getting the ball somewhere on the putting surface—or even out onto shorter grass—may be the best you can hope for. To do so—but only after off-course practice—try the explosion shot, using the sand wedge. Essentially, this is the same stroke you'd play from a green-side bunker. Set up as you would for the sand shot: ball well forward, stance a little open, clubface well open. Then fix your eyes on a point an inch or so behind the ball, pick the club up abruptly with your hands and wrists and hit equally abruptly and *very firmly* with the right hand down into the grass behind the ball at the point you are looking at. Try not to let your left wrist break down through impact, or your right hand roll over your left. The objective is to force the clubhead down through the grass to slide its face under the ball, so you must never baby this shot.

5. Leaves and pine needles can present problems in some areas at certain times of year. You can, of course, try to clean up as much as possible around the ball, but when it is actually balanced above ground on a bed of loose material there is a severe risk of incurring a one-stroke penalty by causing it to move (you also have to replace the ball in its original position, thereby giving yourself the same problem all over again). So be cautious: keep those itchy fingers away and never ground the club at address. Remember that on a full shot you probably won't be able to "grip" the ball on the clubface as cleanly as you'd like, which will make it fly lower and run farther, so go to a more-lofted club. For a short or high pitch, use the explosion technique I just described: ball forward, clubface open, abrupt backswing and downswing, hitting about an inch behind the ball. You don't need as much force here as you do from heavy rough but be firm.

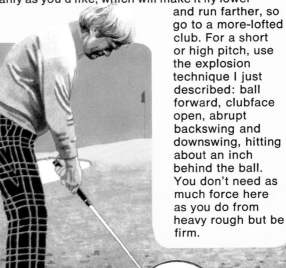

Taming Those Tight Lies

1. Frightened of tight lies? Here's the antidote. Take 20 balls and your 5-iron and 4-wood to the barest piece of hard-pan you can find on the driving range. Beginning with the 5-iron, move the ball an inch or so farther back in your stance while keeping your hands in their normal address position. This will set your hands well ahead of the clubface. From there, make your normal backswing, then hit FIRMLY DOWN into the ball, trying to catch its upper back area before the clubhead touches the ground. Feel as though you are *punching* the clubface down into the ball with firm wrists and your left hand always leading the clubhead. Repeat nine more times with the 5-iron. Then hit 10 shots with your 4-wood using exactly the same technique. This little exercise teaches you the first fundamental for taming every type of tight lie: to get the ball up in the air from a bare lie, you must hit abruptly DOWN on the ball. If you've been missing these shots, it's likely you've been allowing your instincts to control your swing and trying to get the ball in the air by scooping or sweeping at it. That simply won't work, because the result almost always is hitting with the leading edge of the club and a badly skulled shot.

2. On full shots good golfers can get adequate height from many tight lies simply by meeting the ball cleanly with great clubhead speed. The better tour players almost always prefer a bare lie to a fluffy one on a critical approach shot because of the increased backspin they can impart to the ball. If you're not that confident of your striking ability, here's an easier way to get extra height and bite from a tight lie. Put a little cut-spin on the ball and fade it into the target. Set the ball a little farther back in your stance than normal to again promote the hitting-down action, but aim yourself left of target and open the clubface. Make your normal backswing, then, coming through, try to delay the roll of your right hand over your left until well beyond impact. Take plenty of club and, as always when the ball sits tight, look hard at its upper rear section until it vanishes from sight. You can use this technique with all the fairway woods and irons, but it's easiest with the more-lofted woods and the middle irons.

3. Landing in a divot mark is always irritating, but it's not the end of the world and it need not cost you if you use your eyes and your wits. First, look carefully at your target and determine if there is a way to run the ball onto the green without too much risk. If there is such an opportunity, play a punch shot: use at least one more club than normal, choke down, set the ball back a little in your stance with your hands well ahead of it, swing compactly, hit down abruptly with the left hand leading until well past impact, and allow for some draw. If the ball has to be flown all the way to the green, play a cut shot. Take plenty of club, open the face and your address, swing fully, and hit down hard with your right hand without letting it roll over your left until the ball is well on its way. Because of their rounded soles, the lofted woods are ideal for this type of shot, so prefer them over your irons, even if that means choking well down on the club to reduce its distance potential. And, of course, always allow for a fade.

4. If you miss greens on dry courses you'll often be confronted with the need to play a short pitch over some sort of obstacle from hardpan or other type of very close lie. This is one of the toughest shots in the game, so Rule 1 is don't be overambitious: make the putting surface your target rather than the hole. To play this shot most amateurs generally select the pitching wedge or 9-iron and try to nip the ball cleanly—and very frequently they either stick those sharp-edged clubs in the ground or flinch and "blade" the shot way too far. If that's you, then try my technique. Take your sand wedge, aim about a half inch behind the ball, keep your head very still, swing normally, and hit *down* and through firmly without any wrist flipping. If you catch the ball cleanly, well and good. However, if you catch the ground first, the protruding flange of the sand wedge often will allow it to skid and slide under the ball, as in a bunker shot.

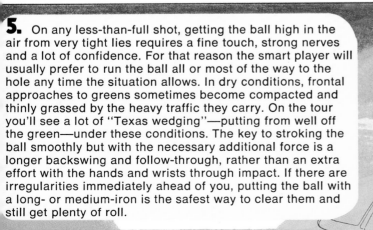

5. On any less-than-full shot, getting the ball high in the air from very tight lies requires a fine touch, strong nerves and a lot of confidence. For that reason the smart player will usually prefer to run the ball all or most of the way to the hole any time the situation allows. In dry conditions, frontal approaches to greens sometimes become compacted and thinly grassed by the heavy traffic they carry. On the tour you'll see a lot of "Texas wedging"—putting from well off the green—under these conditions. The key to stroking the ball smoothly but with the necessary additional force is a longer backswing and follow-through, rather than an extra effort with the hands and wrists through impact. If there are irregularities immediately ahead of you, putting the ball with a long- or medium-iron is the safest way to clear them and still get plenty of roll.

J McQueen

Playing from Angled Lies

1. Strategy No. 1 for dealing with angled lies is to avoid them as much as possible by driving and laying up to the most level fairway areas. This is one reason you will often see me teeing off with less than a driver. I'd almost always rather hit a longer club into a green than approach it from a severely angled lie. This is also the reason I seek the most level area I can find for all tee shots. Strategy No. 2, when you can't avoid uneven lies, is to accept them as a basic part of the game and get on with meeting their special challenge, rather than bemoaning your bad luck or cursing the design of the course. Meeting the challenge requires knowledge of the flight patterns produced by angled lies, and the adjustments necessary to deal with them. Let's look at the four main ones.

NO. 9
392 YDS
par 4

2. Uphill Lie. The ball will fly higher and thus not so far than from level ground, so give yourself sufficient club. You will have a tendency to stay or even fall back on your right foot through impact, which promotes a pull or pull hook to the left, so plan accordingly. The more severe the uphill slope, the harder it becomes to counteract both these effects, so make ample allowances and don't be overambitious. On a really steep uphill lie, be certain to take a club with sufficient loft to clear the top of the hill or mound, even if that means laying up. To offset the effect of the slope as much as possible, set up as perpendicular to it as you can, thereby encouraging a clubhead arc through impact that matches rather than fights the slope. To avoid swaying on the backswing or losing balance swinging through, restrict your body turn a little and swing more with your hands and arms. There's an instinctive tendency to rush these shots, so think "smooth." Don't worry about making a full follow-through.

3. **Downhill Lie.** When the angle is severe this can be the toughest shot in the game, even for the best shotmakers. The ball will tend to fly lower and thus farther and "hotter" than normal. Because you will have difficulty getting the weight off your left side going back and a tendency to sway with the slope coming through, the ball often will be pushed or push-sliced to the right, so allow for that. The longer-shafted the club the shallower its arc through impact and thus the tougher it becomes to avoid catching ground before ball. On really acute downhill slopes, it pays to favor the shorter-shafted, more lofted clubs even at the expense of laying up. Again, the more perpendicular you can set up at address the better your chance of matching the clubhead arc to the slope. Setting most of your weight on your right foot and keeping it there throughout the swing will help prevent swaying or falling forward, as will swinging more with your arms and less with your body. Think "smooth" again, and really try to stay down on this shot; try for a feeling of "chasing" the ball with the clubhead well beyond impact.

4. **Ball Above Feet.** The higher the ball lies relative to your feet, the more erect you should stand at address to give yourself maximum swinging room. Standing more erect will move you farther away from the ball, so choke down on the club until you are a comfortable distance from it. Setting and keeping your weight more toward your toes can help you retain balance on a severe slope. Try to swing compactly and smoothly, allowing the club to move naturally on the flatter plane established by your more erect posture, which will help you to sweep the ball away rather than digging for it. The ball will always tend to hook from this type of lie; you can either allow for this in aiming, or modify the right-to-left curve by opening the clubface at address. If you prefer opening the clubface, take at least one more club to offset the higher flight this will create.

5. **Ball Below Feet.** Getting and staying well "down" to the shot is the chief problem here. Solve it on a slight incline by increasing your knee bend to produce more of a "sitting" posture. This will have the effect of moving your weight more to your heels. Grip the club near the end to help bring yourself as close as possible to normal distance from the ball. On severe slopes you will probably need to lean over more from the hips in addition to increasing your knee bend. Swing compactly and as smoothly as possible, chiefly with your hands and arms; try to retain your knee bend and angle of inclination from the waist right through impact; and keep your head still—any upper-body sway here can easily result in a shank. Shots from this type of lie tend to fade or slice. If you must attempt a straight shot, close the clubface a little and move the ball back in your stance an inch or two—but allow for a lower flight than normal.

J. McQueen

Surviving Odd Obstacles

As a youngster growing up in Ohio I played mainly on lush courses in largely windless conditions, which meant that the ball generally stopped pretty close to where you hit it. Rough was my biggest bugaboo in those days, but an upright swing and a somewhat bulldozing attitude usually got me free of all but the tallest species. Then, when I got out on the pro tour, with its huge variety of course types and ground and weather conditions, it suddenly hit me how much I still had to learn about golf. Lesson No. 1 was the need for imagination rather than brute force in surviving my own mistakes and the inevitable bad bounces that are such a feature of the game. Lesson No. 2 was the need for the special shotmaking skills that would allow me to implement what I imagined. Here are seven situations included in the resulting educational process—a process, I might add, that still continues every time I play or practice.

1. The restricted swing. Playing from under tree limbs and other swing restrictors isn't as difficult as it might seem, given three conditions. First, acclimatize yourself to the feel of the restricted action by properly "measuring" it with plenty of practice swings. Second, forget the obstacle and concentrate on swinging as slowly and smoothly as possible. Third, prevent the anxious peeking that always wrecks these shots by really looking hard at the ball until it vanishes from sight. Also, don't give up in these situations too quickly even when there is no room to make any kind of normal backswing. I've saved many a stroke over the years simply by bumping the ball clear with my putter.

2. The southpaw recovery. Given a reasonable lie, consider a left-handed swing if there is no other way to attack the ball. Take a well-lofted iron—say a 6, 7 or 8—and turn the blade upside down so you can hit with the face of the club, not the back. Reverse your hands to make a left-hander's grip, and take plenty of practice swings to get as much feel as possible for the southpaw action. Then watch the ball closely and try not to rush the stroke. Unless you're ambidextrous, you shouldn't try for too much distance on a shot like this —simply making decent contact to get clear of the obstacle is the best objective. Use your putter and just bump the ball out left-handed, if anything else seems too difficult or risky.

3. The water shot. Extracting a ball that's more than about half an inch under water is a tough assignment, so use common sense and don't risk compounding the original error. If the ball is only that deep or partly above the water, start by putting on your rain gear—that will help reduce the tendency to flinch or quit on the shot that naturally results from the prospect of getting wet. Next, make sure of solid footing, even if that means removing shoes and socks and rolling up the pants. On the shot, pick the club up abruptly and hit down steeply and hard into the water a little farther behind the ball than you instinctively would —much the same as playing from a buried lie in sand.

4. **The bump and run.** Here's a shot you'll frequently see on the pro tour when nothing else will work, especially from a close lie to a tight pin position when mounds or a hard-surfaced bunker intervene. To play it through sand take a long iron, choke down, position the ball back near your right foot with your hands well forward, and make a firm descending blow. This is really a desperation shot, but practice will improve your success ratio. In your practice, include hitting some shots into the sides of mounds, using a medium iron, to get some feel for how much speed various degrees of slope take off the ball.

5. **Fenced in.** There are two possibilities here. The easiest is simply to bump the ball between your legs by beating straight down on top of it with a well-lofted iron. For a more adventurous effort, take two clubs less than you'd need from the fairway, close the clubface acutely, look hard at the ball, and swing normally. If you manage to make clean contact, the severely closed clubface will direct the ball well left and away from the fence, rather than in the direction of the swing. Allow for a low flight and lots of roll.

7. **The ditch-digger.** The lower the ball in relation to where you can stand, the riskier the shot, thus the more you should weigh taking a drop and unplayable lie penalty against having to ditch-dig all over again—and again. If you decide to take the chance, get as close to the ball as you can by bending your knees and leaning over from the waist; swing the club up sharply with a quick wrist-break and then punch the clubhead straight down into the ball. Keep your head and upper body as still as possible and don't worry about a follow-through.

6. **Golf on the rocks.** Hitting off stones obviously imperils your equipment, and it also can damage your eyes, so don't be foolhardy. If you decide to take the risk, and the surface is loose and gravelly, try a bunker-type shot, hitting very firmly down about an inch or two behind the ball. If the rocks are boulder-size, your only chance is to try to nip the ball cleanly. This frequently results in further rock trouble, so consider your other options carefully before trying it.

J. McQueen

Lesson 42:

Some Thoughts on Winning

1. Golf's like everything else in life: you get out of it what you put in. I proved that to myself again in 1979, my worst year since turning pro. At the time I thought I was preparing fully for each tournament I entered, but in retrospect I realize that the effort wasn't quite 100 percent. I worked at the game, but I didn't work hard enough. Perhaps subconsciously, after 25 years of being pretty successful at golf, I thought I could get by on natural talent plus experience. I proved to myself, embarrassingly, that I couldn't. Confidence is the most important single factor in this game and, no matter how great your natural talent, there is only one way to obtain and sustain it: work. That can be a hard fact to swallow, but doing so is the first step to excellence. What I really proved to myself again in 1979 is that there aren't any shortcuts to winning at golf.

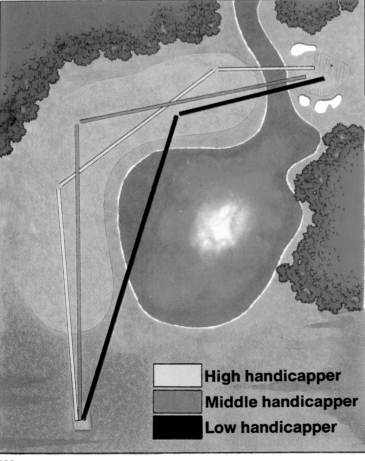

☐ **High handicapper**

☐ **Middle handicapper**

■ **Low handicapper**

2. Confidence in your technique—in your ability to hit the shots—is obviously the first goal of working at the game, but it's not the only kind of confidence you need to translate that skill into winning scores. Equally important is your confidence in strategical and tactical decisions. If you lack conviction in the shot you are about to attempt, no matter how fine your technique, you are bound to swing or stroke tentatively. One of the great weaknesses of handicap players is their lack of conviction about what they are really trying to do with the ball, and it seems to me the chief cause is inadequate planning. Give an engineer a bridge to build and he'll go to the ends of the earth to come up with the right plan, because he knows everything depends upon it. Give him a golf club, however, and he'll hit the ball almost before you've got time to step out of the way. Firing at random may be fun on the driving range, but it's highly unproductive on the course if you play this game to win. If you fail *before you drive* to map out your easiest and safest route from tee to cup, you will always—repeat, *always*—score worse than you swing.

4. Your opponents in golf aren't other people, as in most sports—they are you yourself and the golf course. In my time on the tour there have been dozens of players with marvelous shotmaking skills who failed to win because they couldn't discipline or dedicate themselves sufficiently. Conversely, there have been a number of golfers with such high levels of self-control and commitment that they have been able to win regularly with only average physical abilities. And there is one other strong quality about this second group: they are all great odds-calculators, all great analysts of the highest percentage shot. Unlike the headstrong, gambling types, they recognize and base their games around the fact that most golf courses succumb far more readily to guile and dexterity than to aggression and force. Patience and perseverance, more than their ball-striking capabilities, are their winning weapons.

3. Golf is full of paradoxes, and one of the most important to learn is that the more you let yourself think about winning—when actually competing—the less your chance of doing so. I'm fortunate that I've always been able to enjoy the *effort* of trying to win as much as the result when I've succeeded. That kind of temperament enables me to exist on the golf course almost entirely in the present—to focus totally on each shot without those distractions that can eat away at the nerves when the mind starts trying to anticipate the future. I don't have any easy answers for those who have trouble concentrating on the present when victory seems within reach, but here are a couple of suggestions. First, try your darndest to play *one shot at a time,* never looking back or forward until the final putt is holed. Second, keep in the back of your mind that, win or lose, the sun will rise again tomorrow.

5. As I said at the start, there are no short-cuts to winning at golf, but here's a 10-point plan that I think could help many handicap players. 1. Learn the fundamentals of a good swing and putting stroke and stick to them through thick and thin. 2. Practice more than you play—and especially the short game. 3. Play yourself and the course—never the man or the field. 4. Play to a plan on every hole, and be totally realistic about your own capabilities and the prevailing conditions in making it. 5. Keep your cool —accept the fact that golf never was meant to be a 100 percent fair game, and that you are human and therefore fallible. 6. Don't compound your errors or unlucky breaks—be conservative in your recovery strategy. 7. Live in the present—think about and play only one shot at a time. 8. Play your hardest from the first tee—golf is an 18-hole game, not a one-shot or a one-hole contest. 9. Never hit a "quit" shot, even in practice—and keep trying *whatever happens.* 10. Whether you win or lose, *enjoy* the experience of competing.

Lifetime Records

Professional Career in Capsule
(through 1980)

Total victories around the world 86
Official U.S. tour victories 68
Second place or ties 45
Third place or ties 31

- Career Winnings through 1980 (official tour money): $3,581,213
- Top Money Winner, 1964, 1965, 1967, 1971, 1972, 1973, 1975, 1976.
- PGA Player of the Year Award, 1967, 1972, 1973, 1975, 1976.
- "Major championship" titles, 19: Masters (5); U.S. Open (4); PGA Championship (5); British Open (3); U.S. Amateur (2).
- U.S. Tour career scoring average: 70.4 strokes per round.
- Named "Athlete of the Decade" for the 1970s.

International Victories
- British Open (3): 1966, 1970, 1978 (runner-up seven times)
- Australian Open (6): 1964, 1968, 1971, 1975, 1976, 1978
- World Cup: winner of individual championship a record three times (1963, 1964, 1971) and six times a member of winning U.S. teams (1963, 1964, 1966, 1967, 1971, 1973)
- Ryder Cup: member of U.S. teams 1969, 1971, 1973, 1975, 1977.

Helped into the Augusta National green coat, symbol of Masters champions, in 1963, by previous year's winner Arnold Palmer.

1970 British Open at St. Andrews with wife Barbara on hand for the trophy presentation.

1975 PGA Championship at Firestone, Nicklaus' fourth.   *1980 U.S. Open at Baltusrol.*

Major Championship Record

Year	Masters	U.S. Open	PGA Championship	British Open
1962	Tied 15th	Won	Tied 3rd	Tied 32nd
1963	Won	Missed cut	Won	3rd
1964	Tied 2nd	Tied 23rd	Tied 2nd	2nd
1965	Won	Tied 31st	Tied 2nd	Tied 12th
1966	Won	3rd	Tied 22nd	Won
1967	Missed cut	Won	Tied 3rd	2nd
1968	Tied 5th	2nd	Missed cut	Tied 2nd
1969	Tied 24th	Tied 25th	Tied 11th	Tied 6th
1970	8th	Tied 49th	Tied 6th	Won
1971	Tied 2nd	2nd	Won	Tied 5th
1972	Won	Won	Tied 13th	2nd
1973	Tied 3rd	Tied 4th	Won	4th
1974	Tied 4th	Tied 10th	2nd	3rd
1975	Won	Tied 7th	Won	Tied 3rd
1976	Tied 3rd	Tied 11th	Tied 4th	Tied 2nd
1977	2nd	Tied 10th	3rd	2nd
1978	7th	Tied 6th	Missed cut	Won
1979	4th	Tied 9th	Tied 65th	Tied 2nd
1980	Tied 33rd	Won	Won	Tied 4th
Total	**Won five** **2nd three times** **3rd twice**	**Won four** **2nd twice** **3rd once**	**Won five** **2nd three times** **3rd three times**	**Won three** **2nd seven times** **3rd three times**

Amateur Career Highlights Year by Year

1950—Age 10
- Started golf and shot 51 for first nine holes ever played

1953—Age 13
- Ohio State Junior Champion (13-to-15-year-olds)
- Columbus Junior Match-Play Champion
- Won three matches in first national championship, the USGA Juniors
- Lost in quarterfinals of Columbus District Amateur

1954—Age 14
- Scioto Junior Club Champion, holing in one for first time in final round
- Columbus Junior Match-Play Champion
- Columbus Junior Stroke-Play Champion
- Medalist in Tri-State (Ohio, Indiana, Kentucky) High School Championship
- Lost in second round of USGA Juniors
- Finalist in Columbus District Amateur
- Lost in first round of Ohio State Amateur (won by Arnold Palmer)
- Played on Upper Arlington High School team

1955—Age 15
- Columbus Junior Match-Play Champion
- Columbus Junior Stroke-Play Champion
- Ohio Jaycees winner
- Tied for medalist in National Jaycees
- Lost in quarterfinals of USGA Juniors
- Columbus District Amateur Champion
- Medalist in Ohio State Amateur
- Qualified for U.S. Amateur for first time, losing in first round

1956—Age 16
- Ohio State Junior Champion
- Medalist in Tri-State High-School Championship
- Ohio Jaycees winner
- Lost play-off in National Jaycees
- Lost in semifinals of USGA Juniors
- Lost in quarterfinals of Ohio State Amateur
- Ohio State Open Champion
- Fifth in Sunnehanna Amateur Invitational
- Lost in third round of U.S. Amateur

1957—Age 17
- Central Ohio High School District Champion
- Ohio High Schools State Champion
- Ohio Jaycees winner
- National Jaycees winner
- Lost in third round of USGA Juniors
- Qualified for U.S. Open for first time, missing cut by ten shots with 160
- Lost in fourth round of U.S. Amateur

1958—Age 18
- Trans-Mississippi Champion
- Shot 67-66-76-68 for twelfth place in first pro tour tournament, the Rubber City Open
- Finished in U.S. Open for first time, in forty-first place
- Lost in second round of U.S. Amateur to Harvie Ward, one down

1961 U.S. Amateur at Pebble Beach with runnerup Dudley Wysong.

1959—Age 19

- North-South Amateur Champion
- Played in first Masters, missing cut by one shot with 150
- Played in first Walker Cup Match, winning foursomes and singles matches
- Won Royal St. George's Challenge Vase (England)
- Lost in quarterfinals of British Amateur
- Trans-Mississippi Champion
- Qualified for U.S. Open, missing cut with 154
- U.S. Amateur Champion

1960—Age 20

- International Four-Ball winner (with Deane Beman)
- Tied for low amateur and thirteenth place overall in Masters
- Runner-up in Big Ten Championship
- Runner-up to Arnold Palmer in U.S. Open by two strokes after leading with six holes to play
- Lost in second round of NCAA Championship
- Won both singles and both foursomes matches in first Americas Cup appearance
- Lost in fourth round of U.S. Amateur
- Medalist in World Amateur Team Championship with 66-67-68-68—269 at Merion, leading U.S. team victory

1961—Age 21

- Western Amateur Champion
- Low amateur and tied for seventh in Masters
- Tied for thirty-eighth in Colonial National Invitational (PGA event)
- Tied for fourth in U.S. Open
- NCAA Champion
- Tied for twenty-third in Buick Open (PGA event)
- Tied for fifty-fifth in American Golf Classic (PGA event)
- Won Walker Cup foursomes and singles matches
- U.S. Amateur Champion for second time
- Won both foursomes and halved both singles in Americas Cup matches
- Turned professional November 8

Practicing at Scioto C. C., Columbus, Ohio, age 13.

Professional Career Highlights Year by Year

Out of the rough at Troon during 1962 British Open.

1962 Highlights

Official U.S. tour victories and winnings at each:

U.S. Open	$15,000
Seattle Open	4300
Portland Open	3500

Runner-up in three tournaments, third four times. Official winnings for year: $61,868.95 for third place.

- Won $33.33 in first professional tournament, the Los Angeles Open.
- Won the World Series of Golf eight months later, earning $50,000.
- Won first pro title, defeating Arnold Palmer in playoff for the U.S. Open. Youngest-ever winner of the U.S. Open.
- Won back-to-back tournaments at Seattle and Portland.
- Won money in all twenty-six tournaments entered.
- Named Rookie of the Year for 1962.

1963 Highlights

Official U.S. tour victories and winnings at each:

Masters	$20,000
PGA Championship	13,000
Tournament of Champions	13,000
Sahara Invitational	13,000
Palm Springs Classic	9000

Runner-up in two tournaments, third three times. Official winnings for year: $100,040 for second place.

- Won individual championship at World Cup in Paris, teaming with Arnold Palmer to win the event for the United States.
- Again won the World Series of Golf, earning $50,000.
- Became youngest-ever winner of the Masters, by 1 shot over Tony Lema.
- Finished third in British Open after bogeying last two holes.
- Won PGA Championship by 2 strokes.

Watery lie experienced during 1965 Canadian Open.

1964 Highlights

Official U.S. tour victories and winnings at each:

Whitemarsh Open	$24,042
Tournament of Champions	12,000
Phoenix Open	7500
Portland Open	5800

Runner-up in six tournaments, third three times. Official winnings for year: $113,284.50 for first place.

- Won Australian Open in playoff with Bruce Devlin.
- Won individual championship in World Cup in Hawaii, teaming with Arnold Palmer to win the event for the United States.
- Runner-up in British Open at St. Andrews, breaking record for final thirty-six holes with 66-68.
- Achieved best stroke average on tour with 69.9.
- Money winnings victory represented a margin of $81.13 over Palmer.

1965 Highlights

Official U.S. tour victories and winnings at each:

Masters	$20,000
Philadelphia Classic	24,300
Thunderbird Classic	20,000
Memphis Open	9000
Portland Open	6600

Runner-up in four tournaments, third twice. Official winnings for year: $140,752.14 for first place.

- Won money winnings title for second year, with record total.
- Won Masters title with record score of 271, breaking Ben Hogan's 1953 total by 3 strokes. Also tied course record with 64 in third round.
- Achieved top stroke average for second consecutive year with 70.1.
- Won Portland Open for third time and Philadelphia (Whitemarsh) title second year in a row.
- Took second place in World Series of Golf and also in the individual World Cup honors in Madrid.

Chip with putter to 18th green at Augusta in 1966 Masters.

1966 Highlights

Official U.S. tour victories and winnings at each:

Masters	$20,000
Sahara Invitational	20,000
National Team Championship (with Arnold Palmer)	25,000

Runner-up in three tournaments, third three times. Official winnings for year: $111,419.16 for second place.

- Won British Open at Muirfield, Scotland, becoming the fourth and youngest golfer to win the four major titles (Masters, U.S. Open, PGA, British Open.)
- Became the first back-to-back winner of the Masters after a playoff with Tommy Jacobs and Gay Brewer.
- With Arnold Palmer established a team record of 32 under par in National Team Championship.
- Teamed with Arnold Palmer to win the World Cup in Tokyo for the United States.
- Reached the half-million mark in official career winnings.
- After five years as a professional had never finished lower than third in final money standings, and had finished in the money 110 times out of 114 tour starts.

1967 Highlights

Official U.S. tour victories and winnings at each:

U.S. Open	$30,000
Westchester Classic	50,000
Sahara Invitational	20,000
Western Open	20,000
Crosby National	16,000

Runner-up in two tournaments, third three times. Official winnings for year: $188,998.08 for first place.

- Sank a 22-foot putt on the final green at Baltusrol to break Ben Hogan's U.S. Open record of 1948 with 275.
- Captured the Professional Player of the Year award in his first year of eligibility as PGA member.
- Finished one shot behind winner at PGA Championship and two behind at British Open.
- Won Sahara event for third time, shooting a career-low round of 62.
- Won the World Series of Golf for the third time.
- Winning $50,000 in World Series, plus the same amount at Westchester, gave him $100,000 in a twelve-day period.
- Set new records in money winnings: $188,998.08 official and $261,566.66 unofficial earnings.
- Teamed with Arnold Palmer to win the World Cup in Mexico City for the fourth time.

Teeing off in wind on the formidable 16th at Cypress Point, 1967 Crosby.

133

Short putt drops during 1968 British Open at Carnoustie.

1968 Highlights

Official U.S. tour victories and winnings at each:

Western Open	$26,000
American Golf Classic	25,000

Runner-up in three tournaments, third once.
Official winnings for year: $155,285.55 for second place.

- Won Australian Open for second time, setting course record 64 in second round.
- Won longest playoff of year, defeating Lee Elder at fifth hole in American Golf Classic, Frank Beard being eliminated at first extra hole.
- Won back-to-back tournaments at Western Open and American Classic, and tied for second at Westchester, winning $71,416 in three-week period in August.
- Achieved runner-up spot in three national Opens: U.S., Canadian, and British.

Head to head with Tony Jacklin in 1969 Ryder Cup matches.

1969 Highlights

Official U.S. tour victories and winnings at each:

Andy Williams—	
San Diego Open	$30,000
Kaiser Invitational	28,000
Sahara Invitational	20,000

Runner-up in one tournament.
Official winnings for year: $140,167.42 for third place.

- Approached the million-dollar mark and became second in all-time career earnings with $996,524.17 after eight years as a pro.
- Won the Sahara event for the fourth time.
- Won the Kaiser after a sudden-death playoff against three others.
- Late-season surge earned $62,300 in three consecutive events: wins at Sahara and Kaiser and second place in Hawaiian Open.
- By end of season had lost twenty pounds in weight and six inches off hips.

1970 Highlights

Official U.S. tour victories and winnings at each:

Byron Nelson Classic	$20,000
National Team Championship	20,000
(with Arnold Palmer)	

Runner-up in three tournaments, third twice.
Official winnings for year: $142,148 for fourth place.

- Won British Open for second time after eighteen hole playoff with Doug Sanders at St. Andrews.
- Won World Series of Golf and $50,000 check for a record fourth time.
- Won Piccadilly World Match Play Championship at Wentworth, England.
- Defeated Arnold Palmer on first extra hole in Byron Nelson Classic.
- Teamed with Palmer to win National Team Championship for second time with score of 25 under par.
- Won $76,400 in non-U.S.-tour events.

1971 Highlights

Official U.S. tour victories and winnings at each:

PGA Championship	$40,000
Tournament of Champions	33,000
Disney World Open	30,000
Byron Nelson Classic	25,000
National Team Championship (with Arnold Palmer)	20,000

Runner-up in three tournaments, third three times. Official winnings for year: $244,490.50 for first place.

- With victory in the PGA championship, became first golfer to capture the four major championships twice each.
- Established new money winnings record, bringing his official career total to almost $1,400,000.
- Teamed with Arnold Palmer to win the National Team Championship for the third time.
- Won Tournament of Champions for third time (by 8 strokes).
- Late-season surge included four wins in five starts: Australian Open (by 8 strokes); Australian Dunlop (by 7 strokes); World Cup individual honors (by 7 strokes); Disney World Open (by 3 strokes).
- Teamed with Lee Trevino to win the World Cup in Florida for the United States for a record third time.
- Tied Trevino in U.S. Open, losing playoff 68-71.
- Tied for second in Masters, two strokes behind the winner.

1972 Highlights

Official U.S. tour victories and winnings at each:

Bing Crosby	$28,000
Doral Eastern Open	30,000
Masters	25,000
U.S. Open	30,000
Westchester Classic	50,000
U.S. Professional Match Play Championship	40,000
Disney World Open	30,000

Runner-up in three tournaments.
Official winnings for year: $320,542 for first place.

- Finished second in British Open at Muirfield after final round 66, one shot behind Lee Trevino.
- Won $90,000 in a seventeen-day period by taking the Westchester Classic for the second time, and winning his first U.S. Professional Match Play Championship.
- Won seven tournaments out of nineteen U.S. events entered.
- Established new one-year money-winning record of $320,542, bringing his all-time official earnings to $1,981,830.
- Won Masters for fourth time.
- Won U.S. Open for third time.
- Repeated his victory in the Disney World Open with a 19-under-par total of 267, giving him a 9-stroke margin over runner-up Bobby Mitchell.

Short pitch into 6th at La Costa during 1972 Tournament of Champions.

Long iron off 17th in 1972 U.S. Open at Pebble.

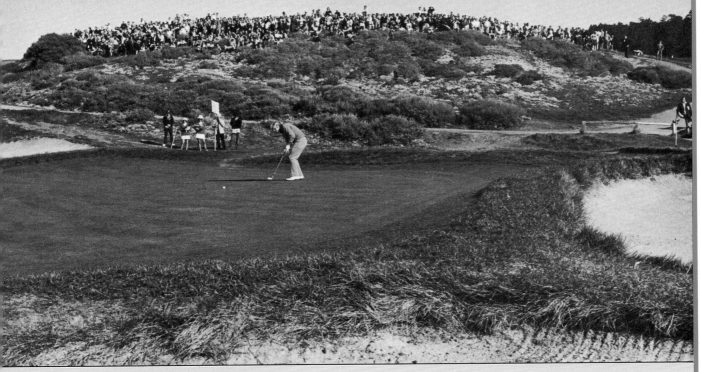

Lag putt on 7th at Pebble Beach, 1972 Crosby.

Long-iron shot during first round of 1973 British Open at Troon.

1973 Highlights

Official U.S. tour victories and winnings at each:

Greater New Orleans Open	$25,000
Bing Crosby	36,000
Atlanta Classic	30,000
Tournament of Champions	40,000
PGA Championship	45,000
Ohio Kings Island Open	25,000
Disney World Open	30,000

Runner-up in one tournament.
Official earnings: $308,124 (leading money-winner); first man in golf to surpass $2,000,000 in all-time official earnings.

- Won third PGA Championship.
- Surpassed Bobby Jones' record on August 12 with PGA Championship victory, his 14th major championship win.
- Out of seventeen tour events entered in 1973, won seven and finished 15 times in the top ten, 13 times in the top six.
- Finished fourth in the British Open, breaking the Troon course record with a seven-under-par 65 in the final round.
- Won fifty-first U.S. tour victory.
- Teamed with John Miller to win the World Cup in Marbella, Spain for the sixth time.

Delicate escape out of greenside bunker at second hole of Augusta National, 1975 Masters.

1974 Highlights

Official U.S. tour victories and winnings at each:

Hawaiin Open	$44,000
Tournament Players Championship	50,000

Finished second in The Colonial National and in the PGA Championship.
Official tour earnings: $236,520; all-time official earnings now surpass $2,500,000.

- Out of eighteen tour events entered in 1974, he finished in the top ten 13 times, 8 times in the top six.

1975 Highlights

Official U.S. tour victories and winnings at each:

Doral Eastern Open	$30,000
Heritage Classic	40,000
Masters	40,000
PGA Championship	45,000
World Open	40,000

Runner-up in one tournament.
Official earnings including non-tour events: $330,123; all-time earnings now surpass $2,750,000.

- In non-tour appearances, won the Australian Open.
- Tied with Tom Weiskopf for Canadian open, lost on first extra hole play-off.
- In nineteen appearances including non-tour events, won six, and finished 17 times in the top ten.
- Shot 30 out of 64 tour rounds in the 60s.
- Named PGA Player of the Year for the fourth time to tie Ben Hogan.
- Registered his 15th and 16th "major championships" wins with a record fifth at Masters, and the PGA Championship for the fourth time. In other "major championships" events of the year, came to within one stroke of first place in British Open and two in the United States Open.

Bunker shot during 1977 British Open play at Turnberry.

1976 Highlights

Official U.S. tour victories and winnings at each:

Tournament Players Championship	$ 60,000
World Series of Golf	100,000

Finished second in Doral-Eastern Open and Canadian Open.

Official tour earnings: $266,438 (leading money-winner).

- Won Australian Open for record fifth time.
- Was top money-winner on U.S. tour for 8th time.
- Placed second in British Open for fifth time.
- Finished in top ten in U.S. tour events 11 times in 16 appearances.
- Named PGA Player of the Year for a record fifth time.

1977 Highlights

Official U.S. tour victories and winnings at each:

Jackie Gleason Inverrary Classic	$50,000
Tournament of Champions	45,000
Memorial Tournament	45,000

Finished second in Masters and Pleasant Valley Classic.

Official tour earnings: $284,509 for second place.

- Became first golfer to win over $3 million on U.S. tour while still being the only player to exceed $2 million in tour winnings.
- Finished second in British Open for sixth time.
- By winning 63rd U.S. tour event overtook Ben Hogan's total and went into second place on all-time victories list behind Sam Snead.
- In 19 appearances, including British Open, finished in top five 11 times and in top ten 15 times.

1978 Highlights

Official U.S. tour victories and winnings at each:

Jackie Gleason Inverrary Classic	$50,000
Tournament Players Championship	60,000
IVB Philadelphia Classic	50,000

Official tour earnings: $256,672 for fourth place.

- Won British Open for third time, bringing major championship victories to 17, and becoming the only man to win all four "majors" at least three times.
- Won Australian Open for a record sixth time.
- Victory in Tournament Players Championship was his third in the five years of that event.
- Victory at Inverrary was his second in a row and was achieved with five straight birdies on the final five holes.
- Named "Sportsman of the Year" by *Sports Illustrated* magazine.

Drive off 5th hole at St. Andrews, one of the trickiest driving holes on the historic course, during 1978 British Open.

1979 Highlights

- Tied for second in British Open, the seventh time he had been runner-up or joint runner-up in world's oldest championship.
- Missed Masters play-off by one stroke, finishing fourth.
- Tied for third in IVB Philadelphia Classic, one stroke behind leaders.
- Major championship record at end of year: 17 victories, 16 seconds, nine thirds, and 58 finishes in the top ten.
- Increased career winnings to $3,408,826 with $85,174 for the year including British Open.
- Was named "Athlete of the Decade" in a nationwide poll of sportswriters, editors and broadcasters.

1980 Highlights

Official U.S. tour victories and winnings at each:

U.S. Open	$55,000
PGA Championship	60,000

Official tour earnings: $175,786, bringing total career winnings to $3,581,213.

- Set new 72-hole record of 272 in winning fourth U.S. Open, plus 36-hole and 54-hole records. Joined Willie Anderson, Bobby Jones and Ben Hogan as only four-time winners of U.S. Open.
- Won fifth PGA Championship, by equaling Walter Hagen's record.
- Became first golfer since Ben Hogan in 1948 to win U.S. Open and PGA Championship in same year.
- Tied for first in Doral-Eastern Open, losing play-off at second extra hole.
- Finished fourth in British Open — the 15th time in 19 attempts he has finished in the top four.

Out of rough at Royal Lytham & St. Annes, 1979 British Open.

...ttle pitch onto 17th green during 1980 U.S. Open, Baltusrol.